THE MAN WITH THE
GOLD ROLODEX

PR To The Stars

David Mirisch & Pierre Patrick

Published in the USA by:
BearManor Media
P O Box 71426
Albany, Georgia 31708
www.bearmanormedia.com

Printed in the United States of America
ISBN   978-1-62933-149-2 (hardcover)

Book & cover design and layout by Darlene Swanson • www.van-garde.com

Contents

Acknowledgements v

What Makes A Star 1

My Life, and What a Life 5

Encounters with the King and the Chairman of the Board 121

David Touring Communist China 129

David Mirisch: Creating Press Path for Pink Panther 133

Hollywood vs. Wives 141

Kids vs. Fame 145

Meeting the Master 147

Acknowledgements

Pierre and David would like to thank some wonderful people who helped make this book journey come true. The incredible staff and crew of "The Jerry Pace Agency" including Ysobelle, Sharon, Serena, Alex, Sarah, Nizeli, Kalechi, Okey, and our more than thousands of clients are always ready for every audition.

Special Thanks goes to Jenna McCombie, Mikel Steven, for their photos and support and to Dante DiBello for his vigilance and attentiveness in putting this book together. Special Thanks also to Jennifer Day and Ron Drake for their encouragement with this endeavor. Special thanks to Joshua McClain and Ben Ronning. To my parents and family for their love and support.

~ Pierre Patrrick

Thanks to these people that have been an important part of my life. My wife and partner for 35 years, Sandy, my three wonderful children Angela, Michael, and Summer, my loving sister Nan, close friends such as Jason Felts, Irwin "Jake" Shorr, Marvin Kramer, Peter Schroeder and David DePatie. Would like to thank as well celebrity friends, Pat Boone, Alan Thicke, Kevin Dobson, Hal Linden and Connie Stevens and many more for always being there. Love you all for being there for me.

~ David Mirisch

What Makes A Star

SINCE THE BEGINNING of time, all of us have taken an evening or two to look at the sky and see dozens, hundreds, thousands and even millions of stars. The ones we know became famous because a long time ago astronomers decided to give them names! Since then, we have seen countless movies on Venus, Jupiter, The Sun and especially Mars, from *My Favorite Martian* to *The Martian* in 2015. Astronomers literally created these stars by looking at the sky.

Looking down on earth, particularly in Hollywood on the sidewalk, we are looking at more than 2,500 stars. All of them had their very own astronomer, creator or star maker.

This book will tell you the story of one of those very special star makers, DAVID MIRISCH, who achieved this by his own unique style of charm, heart, conviction determination, flare and savoir faire. Coming from the Oscar winning Mirisch family, a Hollywood Dynasty, David established himself as a star discoverer, press agent and event maker.

One of his brightest discoveries came directly from the sky. Her name was Farrah Fawcett. He found her after receiving a collection of 8' x 10s" from the University of Texas for a project he was working on. When he saw her face there was something almost angelic about her. He got in touch with a good friend of his, agent Dick Clayton who submitted her to *Screen Gems*. She would become the most popular star in 1976 with *Charlie's Angels*.

Farrah was just one of many of David's special finds. E.J. Peaker, who was one of Broadway's best, a television star (*The Tonight Show*, 25 times) and co-starred with Barbra Streisand in *Hello Dolly*. E.J. was very emotional when talking to us about David and how influential he was in guiding her career. Billboard Chart Topper and T.V. star Gloria Loring and her then husband Alan Thicke praised David for the guidance he gave them in a sometime difficult Hollywood journey.

In an interview for this book, Alan Thicke revealed that his entry to Hollywood was because of David. David, at the time, was helping star Gloria Loring (*Days of our Lives*) as her publicist. Alan gathered great contacts through David's tennis, golf, and events he put together. It gave him assurance to move forward in his career. His first audition was a friendly game of tennis at David's house with David. David realized quickly that Alan had an outstanding personality, was funny, and could play tennis. He quickly started booking him on the fundraising circuit. Alan was eventually given his own talk show in Canada. He produced one of the top-rated variety shows in Canada, *The Rene Simard Show*, and later of course would star in ABC's hit, *Growing Pains*. He and Gloria gave birth to Grammy winning superstar Robin Thicke.

In this book we will take you on a sentimental journey of David Mirisch's career, with never seen historical photos of amazing legends that David worked with. The cavalcade of stars include Frank Sinatra, Peter Sellers, Dionne Warwick, Julie Andrews, Pat Boone, Yogi Berra, Sugar Ray Robinson, John Wayne, Jonathan Winters, James Caan, Jerry Lewis, Duke Ellington, Perry Como, Robert Mitchum, Gary Cooper, Michael Landon, and many more.

We will bring you the beginning of David's career in his own words, and interviews with some chosen participants that include: Robert Wagner, Lyle Waggoner, E.J Peaker, Rebecca Holden, Hal Linden, and many more.

My Life, and What a Life

SEGMENTS:

July 24, 1935 – I was born in Gettysburg, Pennsylvania

We lived in a single-family home in the middle of town. My father was managing two movie theaters. Adam Myers was our "male servant" and Ruby was our "female servant." My sister, Nan, described me as "cute as could be and a devil." She remembers that one time I put stones in my dad's gas tank. I was just being a "normal" kid. My mother, Frances Lewis, was born in Lansing, Michigan. She went to Ramona Convent in Alhambra, a private school for privileged children. My sister Florence (now Nan) was born in Richmond, Virginia and moved to New York City right after she graduated from Shorewood High School in Milwaukee, Wisconsin. She auditioned for numerous plays and did a number of them on Broadway. While doing this, she met Arnold Nodiff (who was a painter) and became a mom. She gave us show business and became a mother of Deborah, Wendy, and Vicky. One of the things Nan remembers was my mom saying, "Don't hit him on the back of his head – you'll make him crazy." We had fun doing this for many years, as it was that little link that brought us back to my childhood.

Milwaukee, Wisconsin

My father and his brothers created Theatres Candy Company in 1944, a candy concession business that grew to encompass 800 movie theaters throughout the Midwest, one of the largest such businesses in the country at that time. My father, Irving, stayed in Milwaukee to run this company, and Harold, Marvin, and Walter headed to Hollywood to enter into the film industry. I attended Atwater Junior High. We lived right across the street from the school. I went to Temple Emanuel. Neither of my parents were very religious and we rarely observed the Jewish holidays. When I was 13, I was supposed to be bar-mitzvahed, but a few weeks before graduation I told my parents I was not going to continue, as in my heart I did not feel I "deserved" the presents, as I really had not properly studied. I was already being a "good guy" at the age of 13. My parents were typical mid-west eaters. Nothing spicy. I don't think we ever ate fish. Our dinners were meat loaf, steak and potatoes, and liver and onions. I remember mom used to make a great Pineapple upside down cake. I remember having a paper route that I used to deliver on my bicycle. I also used to listen to radio shows like *Hopalong Cassidy*, *The Shadow*, *The Green Hornet*, *The Jack Benny Show*, *Burns and Allen*, and *Amos and Andy*." We lived at 1300 E. Lawnwood Place, at the corner of Lawnwood and Ardmore.

Robert Wagner revealed for this book my next school period

David and I went to California Preparatory School for Boys in (1947) David was 4 grades below. It was a beautiful school, wonderful, with a stream that ran through the Ojai Valley right to the Pacific Ocean. It was a rather liberal school and Robert always had the thought of becoming an actor; he always had that ambition. He worked with the Mirisch Family on *The Pink Panther* and *Midway*. He says the Mirisch family was ahead of their time with the best directors and writers; they were never difficult to get along with. Some of the events David put on Robert was a part of. Robert now lives in Colorado with his wife, actress Jill John, and he loves it there.

Camp Indianola - 1943

I was there for 13 summers as a camper and a counselor – Lake Mendota, Madison, Wisconsin.

In 1949 they called me Dave and my nickname was "Mash." At the age of 14, I won my first tennis singles title. My first job on the camp newspaper, *The Totem Pole*, was as circulation manager. I was appointed a Buckskin Head, as voted on by my fellow campers.

In 1951 I was 16 years old and became editor-in-chief of *The Totem Pole*. My friend from Shorewood High School, Billy Olsen, also went there for a few years. He remembered that Orson Wells had gone there a few years before us. These were the very best summers of my early life.

In 1952 I was 17 years old and became a junior counselor after all my years as a camper. I still retained the position of editor-in-chief of *The Totem Pole*. Even then I had a great interest in journalism, which was one of my minors in college.

By 1954 I finally became a full-fledged counselor with my own cabin of 7 boys, aged 9 and 10. Our cabin was called "Pueblo" and I taught various sports on the athletic field – which I was good at.

Comments By Fellow Campers

The year that I started doing my sports scrapbooks, which became my number one hobby, was in 1950. I cut out clippings on baseball, football, and basketball from publications such as *The Milwaukee Journal*, *Sport* magazine, *Sports Illustrated*, and *The Sporting News*. I clipped every record ever set in those three sports. I have clippings from every World Series, Super Bowl, All-Star Game, NBA playoffs, and NCAA college basketball tournaments. I started with regular size books and then realized I needed to go to the biggest that I could buy. I didn't realize when I started doing this that the papers would fade, so somewhere along the way I started to put clear contact paper on them. So, they will now last for an eternity.

As I still keep my scrapbooks up to date, every now and then when I would get with a famous person whose clippings were in my books they would be amazed that I had clippings they had never even seen — like Wilt Chamberlain. I also included in the books pictures of myself with athletes that had set records, like Emmitt Smith and Marcus Allen of the NFL, and basketball All-Americans that I had met at The City of Hope Victor Awards.

Shorewood High School from 1950-1953

I had two nicknames – Mash and Strawberry, as I had strawberry blonde hair. Our house was located on the corner of Ardmore and Lawnwood. For some fun reason the guys called my mother "Frantic Frances." That may have been because one time I was having a party at my house that turned into a snowball fight that moved right inside our house. I vividly remember shoveling more snow than you can imagine. One winter we had it piled up to the top of the front door and I had to make a path to get to the sidewalk to get to the street.

Tom Wegner recalls I had a crush on a girl one year older than myself, by the name of Louise Sander. He said we used to get on our bicycles and ride out to her home, which was at Brown Deer Road and Port Washington Roads. Peter Schroeder and I played on The North Shore Presbyterian Basketball Team. Peter, being the tallest in the group was the leading scorer. I was a guard. I shot two-handed set shots, and, I was a good underhanded free throw shooter. Peter reminded me years later that while we were in 7th grade I taught him to never use the "N" word, as Ruby our maid was an African American. He felt that my lack of prejudice paid off in the future in my dealing with the many African American athletes and celebrities I handled and worked with in my career.

I played on the varsity tennis team. Was a member of the American Junior Bowling Congress, and I set pins and bowled at The Oriental Lanes, The Strachota Milshore Lanes, and the few lanes we actually had at the high school. I was active in Junior Achievement and helped put out their newspaper. Even then, I could throw a football as far as college quarterback – 70 yards. Even further than my friend and the quarterback on the varsity football team, Guy "Punky" Martin, who soon after school married the prettiest girl in the school, Marilyn Johnston. They always say, "The quarterback gets the prettiest girl or top cheerleader." Well, he did. Not sure why I never went out for football. Maybe I was just too busy doing all of my other scholastic and athletic endeavors.

I also wrote for *The Shorewood Herald* and covered high school sports for *The Milwaukee Journal*. I played number 3 and number 2 singles on the tennis team; the number one players were Clint Parsons and Bruce Larkin. Billy Olson remembers "That I once drove a bunch of the guys on the tennis team to a match in Neenah. I got cramps in my legs (which I still get 67 years later) and wouldn't let anyone else drive, so we sat there on the side of the highway until my cramps subsided." I guess it was my dad's car or mine (not sure which), but I didn't want anyone else driving it. Billy also remembers coming to our house for lunch one day and I made him laugh so hard he spit his spaghetti all over the wall. He tells me every time he came over to my house my mom reminded him where the spot was on the wall.

Dick Selby remembers things like when he, Stan Mendelsohn, and Harlan Smith would sleep over at our house. We had a piano and Harlan would play lots of fun tunes. We used to go bowling at the Oriental Lanes, only paying 5 cents per game to give to the pin boys. Then, we would go upstairs on a Saturday afternoon to the Oriental Theatre to get in to see a movie for free and have some of my dad's popcorn, also for free. He also remembers when I was living in Beverly Hills that I invited him to a costume party in Beverly Hills. I got an outfit from Western Costume and Harlan wore his army uniform. He remembers me drinking a lot of Vodka straight out of the bottle (which has always been my choice of alcohol). He remembers a very attractive hostess in a white fur bikini. Funny, the things we remember 60 years later. By coincidence, the upper-flat that Teena and I lived in, he and his wife eventually bought. He also remembered that Teena had a declawed cat that used to like to play with of a fencing foil we had in the house. I can't remember why we had one, but possibly Teena was into that sport.

Tom Wegner reminded me that we used to have lots of basketball games playing across the street from our garage, to the net on Bruce Marshall's net. One of the guys who played in the games was Jimmy Barth, "the midget," who was a few years behind us. Tom also reminded me that I always took the guys free into the Oriental Theatre where we ran the candy stand. I only went with one girl during my two years at Shorewood – Jackie Wolters. She was 5 foot 2 inches, and built as good as a gal could be in those pre-silicon days. I remember that I gave her lots of cashmere sweaters. Tom also remembers my closest friends throwing me a going away party when I had volunteered for the draft during The Korean War. I have pictures standing in front of my house ready for my dad to drive me down to the draft board. Well, I get down there and they said, "Do you have any injuries?" I said that during the summer I had injured my knee while I was in Hawaii while my family was filming *Beachhead* with Tony Curtis, Frank Lovejoy, and Mary Murphy. The cast and crew were playing a softball game against a team made up of locals. I think I injured my knee batting or sliding. So, that was the end of my military career.

My two years in Los Angeles with my parents
I was about 12-13. One year I went to Beverly Vista Junior High and one year I went to California Preparatory School for Boys, in Ojai, California. I had a horse called Dahlia. Actor Robert Wagner was a senior then. I have that school picture in my album. I guess I have been a "collector" for the years from high school on, as I had a stamp collection. Then, I collected match covers from all of the hotels and resorts that we visited throughout the world. I then switched to golf bag tags, and I displayed these first in our wine cellar in the La Costa house and then on the walls of our beach house in Encinitas.

Through the years I collected miniature horses, and at the Encinitas house we had a great glass enclosed cabinet that I put them all on display. One year my wife Sandy entered me into the Del Mar Fair Collectables Division with 400 miniature horse statues, and we brought home a 3rd place ribbon. Many of the horses I picked up on trips and many were given to me by family members and closest friends. About 1990, when we were driving between San Diego and Hemet, I noticed a business that made outdoor statues. We stopped and I saw this beautiful 5-foot white horse. We bought it and they brought it down. We first put it up in the patio of our La Costa home and then put it in our front yard of our home in Encinitas.

My family produced the movie *Beachhead* in 1953 with Tony Curtis, Frank Lovejoy, Mary Murphy, Eduard Franz, Alan Wells, John Doucette, and Skip Homier. Howard W. Koch produced it; it was filmed in Hawaii during my summer break. It was a film taking place at the height of World War II and was the story of four Marines attempting to discover the location of a Japanese minefield. I was brought along to learn the business and do whatever I could. Plus, I had a small part in the film. We scheduled a softball game of our cast and crew against a local team. Well, I went up to bat one time and took a "Casey at the bat" swing and my knee popped right out. My scene was eliminated as I was going to have a small, recurring role. I was immediately shipped back to Los Angeles. Fortunately, no surgery was required but I remember being on crutches for quite a while. My one and only acting debut and I blew it.

Tony Curtis, David Mirisch

I graduated from Shorewood High School

I guess my family and I decided it would be a good idea for me get away from home, so somehow we found The University of Colorado in Boulder, Colorado. At the time, it had a reputation of being one of the biggest party schools in the country, even though I was not a beer drinker and having grown up in the beer capitol of the world – Milwaukee. My first year I lived in Hallett Hall, a dorm for men. My dorm parents were Roger and Sue Hunt. Roger was a blocking back on the CU football team. One of my best friends at that time was Berry Craddock, who would be my roommate for one year. He now lives in Colorado Springs and went on to become a very successful builder and land developer. He said "I was energetic, full of life and loved the girls, particularly the beautiful ones. He said I wouldn't hesitate to ask out any beauty queen even if I just saw her picture in the *Colorado Daily*." Barry remembers that year our family's production of *Moulin Rouge* with Zsa Zsa Gabor, and Jose Ferrer came out. It was a big hit and I took my friends six times to see the film.

That year, one of our friends also took us six nights in a row to see *The Western Stock Rodeo Show*. I also became an un-official member of ZBT fraternity because I had such a great throwing arm (I could throw a football 70 yards); they had me quarterback the frat team and we won the intramural championship. Can't remember why I didn't pledge the fraternity. Maybe, someday, someone will let me know the answer to that question.

Boulder had two popular hangout spots – The Sink and Tulagi's, and I believe one of them is still open today. One of Barry's cousins was a bartender at Tulagi's so we used to get free beer. But, I don't really remember being much of a beer drinker. I never really liked the stuff. I'm glad I never got into it as when I went back to Milwaukee somewhere in the 1980's I bumped into some of my old friends and many of them had "Milwaukee beer belly's."

The last time I saw Berry was in his hometown of Colorado Springs when I did a celebrity event for the ARC, a drug and rehabilitation center. He said I made up a 3x5 foot picture of us from our days at CU that I had brought as a present for him. I started out in general education but started to major in journalism and history. I enjoyed both. Unfortunately, my grades weren't very good and after two years I had a 1.24 GPA. I remember I used to go water skiing at Horsetooth Reservoir in Ft. Collins. I remember we used to go into near-by Denver now and then for an evening out. We had a great football team during my two years there with All-American running backs Carroll Hardy and Frank Bernardi, and a fullback by the name of Johnny Bayuk. Since I didn't drink beer I used to fill up a flask with peppermint schnapps. We also had a college All-American basketball player by the name of "Berdie Halderson." On September 8, 1955, my Uncle Harold sent me a letter (that I have in my file). He gave it to me as I was beginning a new job at 20th Century Fox. Harold told me to take my job seriously, save money, and don't throw my weight around because I was a Mirisch, who were very important people at that time in the film industry. This was between The University of Colorado and Ripon College. I spent that summer going to summer school at The University of Wisconsin in Madison. It was probably the best summer I had ever had up until then. My father gave me money for room and board. I took the money he gave me for board and got a job serving tables at a sorority house. I took the money he gave me for food and rented a water-ski boat. I would go to school in the morning, serve lunch, and then my buddies and I would hop in our ski-boat and go from one sorority pier to another, saying, "Who would like to go water skiing?" I had no lack of dates that summer. I became a good water skier and did it for many years after that on all of the vacations that I went on. I used to ski on one ski and was quite good at it – even if I do say myself.

I met Ken Luber from Milwaukee at Ripon College in 1956. I lived in my fraternity house, Theta Chi. Ken was a Sigma Nu, but they did not have a room there for him so he moved into Theta Chi. He helped me with Spanish. While at Ripon I was number two on the men's tennis team. Ken said, "I was a very friendly guy and a smoozer." Ken and I may have been the only two Jewish boys on campus. He remembered that we went down to Florida on a spring break, and, a travelling rabbi invited us to Oshkosh for Jewish services.

That summer I also went on a student tour to Europe. We went over on the Queen Mary and came back on the Queen Elizabeth. I did have a shipboard romance with a girl by the name of Ann. There were about 25 of us filling up one van. We went to countries like England, France, Belgium, Germany, Switzerland, and Denmark. It was there in Denmark that I lost my virginity. Jackie and I had never "gone all the way" in high school, so the setting was perfect when we got to Amsterdam. They had "houses of ill-repute" all up and down a few streets. I guess the guys in the group picked one out for me and that was that. I remember when we went to Heidelburg, Germany, that I met a beautiful girl by the name of Ursula and we flirted around for a few days.

At Ripon College in 1957 (Ripon, Wisconsin 1956-1959)

I was president of the Student Union Board and I was totally responsible for bringing jazz great pianist Dave Brubeck up for a concert. I was also head cheerleader: Seven beautiful college girls and me. I was quarterback on the Theta Chi Fraternity football team and played on the varsity tennis team. I also had the highest bowling average for two years in a row – 185. One of my former classmates, Bill Popko, reminded me of the following incident. We were on a bus trip to a football game in Carleton, Minnesota. "We were at a red light when I yelled out 'Bus driver, don't move. I dropped my wallet out of the window.' Bob looked out of the window and saw a liquor store and knew what was happening. I turned to the guys on the bus and said, "Quick, give me some money." They did and I dashed out of the bus and into the store and returned with seven half pints of peppermint schnapps, which is what we drank at every game, except when I was acting as head cheerleader. He also remembered that I had free passes to the movies and would take the guys and some of their wives when I could.

In 1958 I graduated from Ripon College with a B.A. in speech. I actually made the Dean's List one semester with a 3.44 GPA.

Our candy concession company had offices around the Midwest in 1959 and I worked under a nice guy by the name of Sidney Rudnick. I spent time in drive-in theatres helping set up the concession stands, and I remember I spent a month living in the Hartford YMCA when I was working in that territory. We went from theaters to discount department stores. One of the chains we worked with was Miracle Mart, and we had locations in a number of cities around the country. Some that I remember were Scranton and York, Pennsylvania. and Odessa/Midland Texas. My job was to hire the help and I remember always choosing attractive young women to as many positions as I could find. I also had to interview different purveyors like bread, milk, ice cream, meats, and hire vegetable and fruit vendors to sell us their products. I think I did this for six months.

I spent a year working for United Artists Pictures as a publicity fieldman. That is where I met Angela's mother, Tina, in St. Louis, Missouri. Working on a picture called *The Devil's Disciple*. I also met

Sharon Waggoner (Lyle Waggoner's wife – he was on *The Carol Burnett Show* and *Wonder Woman*); Sharon was a friend of Tina's. As Lyle reflected on his time with David Mirisch for this book, he commented on David's extraordinary friendship and organization throughout the years they spent together. All the events that Lyle and his wife participated in were "always effectively done thanks to David. David was an extraordinary friend and a joy to work with."

I Married Tina Walsh from St. Louis, Missouri. My first child, Angela Frances, was born on July 23, 1960 at Mt. Sinai Hospital at 4:00 AM. She weighed 7 pounds. 9 ounces, and was 20 ½ inches long. The three of us lived in a duplex in Shorewood. My dad opened up a caramel corn shop for me down on Wisconsin Avenue.

I moved to California in 1960 and spent the first year working for United Artists Pictures as a publicity man.

I then spent a year working as the personal assistant to Henry Rogers, then president of Rogers & Cowan Public Relations (then, the number one theatrical PR firm in Hollywood).

Paul Bloch and Sandy Friedman started when I did and we are still there.

Met Millicent Braverman and I formed Braverman-Mirisch Advertising & Public Relations.

In the 1960's I started doing publicity for some brilliant and beautiful young actresses that went onto fame. They were probably brief campaigns, but I have pictures of the following from those years. Following are the years I worked with them and then the film or series that made them famous amongst numerous films: Karen Black, 1960 (*Five Easy Pieces*); Linda Evans, 1963 (*The Big Valley*); Barbara Eden 1964 (*I Dream of Jeanie*), Mary Ann Mobley 1965 (Elvis Presley films), Beverly Adams, 1965 (married hair stylist Vidal Sasoon);

17

Mariette Hartley, 1965 (Polaroid commercials with James Garner); Barbara Parkins, 1965 (*Peyton Place*); Raquel Welch (*One Million Years B.C*); Barbara Hershey, 1966 (*The Monroes* and *Hannah and Her Sisters*); Ellen Burstyn, 1967 — her name then was Ellen McRae — she went on to win an Academy Award for her role in *Alice Doesn't Live Here Anymore*; Judy Carne, 1968 (Rowan and Martin's Laugh-In *Sock-It-To- Me*); Susan Flannery, 1970, four-time daytime Emmy Award winner for her role on *The Bold and the Beautiful*; Emmy wining Barbara Anderson, 1970 (the television series with Raymond Burr *Ironside*); Tony Award and two-time Emmy Award winner, Jane Alexander; 1970 (*The Great White Hope*); Academy Award winner, Jane Alexander, 1976 (the television series *Dallas*); Also, in 1972, I handled the press for the wedding of Academy Award winner actress Patty Duke and John Astin (*The Addams Family*).

Wife Number Two - Cynthia

I met Cynthia Ann Green, Michael's mother, while she was working as a mermaid at Disneyland. Personal manager Phil Gittelman was our best man and resides today in good health at The Motion Picture and Television Fund in Woodland Hills.

I then bought this big house in Encino with a tennis court and all of the trimmings.

Irwin "Jake" Shorr moved into the guest room and we have remained close friends for all of these years. At this time, I also met my longtime good friend, Marvin Kramer, who passed away in 2016. We were such good friends that he named his son after me.

During these PR years, I represented over 500 actors, actresses and singers.

In 1978 I put together the first Los Angeles Rams cheerleading squad and we have current numbers on 21 of them.

I also put together the Hollywood Celebrity All-Star basketball team. The first year it was all members of the Los Angeles Dodgers. Doug Corbin, Pat Boone's son-in-law, was a member of the team from the second year on.

Braverman-Mirisch

My PR partners after my first partner, Millicent Braverman, were Phil Paladino, Mark Landia, Shelly Saltman, and Steve Simons.

I did PR for 15 years then went into the event business. My first event was for former US Open tennis champion, Tony Trabert, at Murietta Hot Springs.

In 1962 I handled my first major recording artist client, Herb Alpert and The Tijuana Brass. The partners were trumpet player Herb Alpert and his business partner Jerry Moss – thus forming A&M Records. At the time, they had a small office on the second floor of a building on Sunset Boulevard. Their director of operations was the guy I dealt with most of the time, by the name of Gil Friesen. The first album they released was *The Lonely Bull* which became the number one album on all of the national record charts. In the next year or two they moved their offices over to LaBrea and released albums entitled *South of the Border* and *Whipped Cream and Other Delights*. At that time, they were the only recording artists to ever have four albums in the top ten. I still have their first press kit in my files. Herb went on to keep recording and Jerry went into the horse racing business where he won some very big races.

1962 was the first of three years that I worked with the Hollywood makeup artists and hair stylists in putting together *The Hollywood Deb Star Ball* at The Hollywood Palladium. Each of ten major studios selected a girl to view for "Deb Star of The Year." My uncles would allow me to select an actress who would represent The Mirisch Corporation. In 1963 it was Celeste Yarnall, in 1966 it was Phyllis Davis, and 1968 it was Lana Wood. Some of the Deb Stars during those years who went onto fame were Sally Field, Peggy Lipton, Cheryl Miller, and Patty McCormack. It was in 1967-68 that I met my longtime friend E.J.Peaker. She represented Screen Gems, where she was under contract. She hired me to do her publicity after that and she went on to co-star with Barbra Streisand in *Hello Dolly* and with Jon Voight in *The All-American Boy*. We've been best friends ever since.

In 1963 I handled the publicity of a stunning new actress, Anjanette Comer. A young man by the name of Byron Raphael managed her. He was short in stature, but big in ambition. He truly wanted to make her a major star. I remember she was quite shy and really didn't like doing interviews, but she did them because Byron told her to do them. She started out doing some guest star roles on television, and then he got her starring roles with major stars such as Robert Morse (*The Loved One*), Marlon Brandon (*The Apaloosa*), Anthony Quinn (*Guns of San Sebastian*), and Robert Wagner (*Banning*).

We both felt she was on her way. In 1970 she did a picture called *Rabbit Run* with James Caan. Even after all the great press I got her, and starring opposite these big-name stars, she never made it as a big star. Looking back, I think it was because none of these films were a box office hit. If even one of them had been I think she would have gone on to film greatness. I didn't see her for many years, but she did come to my 70th birthday party.

One of the more popular nightclubs in Hollywood was PJ's, located on Santa Monica Blvd. and La Cienega. They had popular jazz artists and singers of that era perform there. One was pianist Eddie

Cano, who used to bring in big crowds. One night I went with some friends and I saw this wonderful Latin artist bringing the crowd to its feet. His name was Trini Lopez. Well, somehow, a personal manager by the name of Bullets Durgom and I got together to handle Trini. Bullets as his manager, and I as his press agent. Bullets signed him to Reprise Records and that year he came out with his hit album *Trini Lopez Live at PJ's*. One of the songs in the album was released as a single. It was called "If I Had a Hammer." It hit number one in 36 countries around the world and went to number 3 in the United States. In 1965 he released "Lemon Tree," 1966 "La Bamba," and also in 1966, "I'm Coming Home Cindy."

I represented Trini for a number of years and had him perform at many of my celebrity fundraising events around the United States. My friend Berry Craddock recalls coming to one of Trini's star-studded opening nights. He said there were beautiful people everywhere in the club with food and drinks open to all of our guests. The kid from Canon City, Colorado had never seen anything like this, and remembers it clearly to this day. In the future, Berry joined me at The Las Vegas Hilton for a few of The Victor Award shows and he remembers me treating him royally and introducing him to Baron Hilton at Mr. Hilton's after-awards reception.

During the 28 years that I was involved in The Victor Awards, Sandy and I brought different couples to be our guests. Like David Sidell, Marvin Kramer, Steve and Menou Ball, Jennifer Josephs and her Michael, Adele and Bob Mathews, Peter and Carolyn Schroeder, and Michael and Vicky Mirisch. And for quite a few years I also invited my former Ripon College friend, Lorenzo "Larry" Doss.

I started to do the PR in 1965 for one of my biggest recording stars, Gary Lewis — son of comedian Jerry Lewis. He had a recording group called *Gary Lewis and The Playboys*. They recorded a song called "This Diamond Ring" that was number one on all the Billboard and Cashbox record lists. That year, Gary was voted by Cashbox Magazine as "The Male Vocalist of the Year," beating out Elvis Presley and Frank Sinatra. He had 8 Gold record singles, 17 top 40 hits, and 4 Gold albums. The first 7 singles he recorded all reached the Top Ten list. Some of his other big hits were "Everybody Loves A Clown," "Count Me In," "Save Your Heart For Me," and She's Just My Style." Gary vividly remembers all of the great publicity things I did for him in the late 60's, especially on our trips to Hawaii where he met his first wife, Jinky Suzara. We danced with hula girls, made Poi, went water skiing, and according to Gary, I even ate Japanese food, which I don't remember as I really don't like it. I went over to the home of his dad, Jerry Lewis, quite frequently. Gary said many of these pictures are in his concert program.

Gary Lewis gets inducted into the US Army, David Mirisch

In 1966 I pulled off one of my two major publicity stunts in my career. Gary was inducted into the United States Army in 1966. I remembered a scene from the movie *Bye Bye Birdie* that starred Ann-Margret, who I had one memorable date where I took her to PJ's nightclub on Santa Monica, to see my client Trini Lopez. In the movie, the lead actor, Conrad Birdie, came to a small town to give a lucky young lady a kiss on national television – on *The Ed Sullivan Show*. So, I used my highly creative mind and I contacted the number one rated television show on the air, *The Ed Sullivan Show*, to see if we could run a contest for some lucky girl to give Gary "his last kiss" before he went into the Army. We ran a national contest and some young teenager from the Midwest by the name of Cyndie Palmer won the contest and gave Gary his last kiss before he went into the Army. That picture turned into a full page spread on the back page of the *New York Daily News*. We held a press conference a day or so before Gary actually went into the service. Once Gary went into the service, my doing PR for him stopped, and that was really the end of our professional relationship.

That year I met Ann Sidney, from England, who had just won the *Miss World* title. I met her just after she finished her tour with Bob Hope. I did quite a bit of publicity for her, including a meeting with then Los Angeles Mayor, Sam Yorty. We took a little lamb with us to his office to promote the British wool industry. I also fixed her up on some dates with the cowboy actor, Ty Hardin. I also set it up for her to visit the set of the television series *The Munsters*, where she met the star of the show, Yvonne De Carlo.

Ken Luber came back from India and stayed with me for a few months at my house on Hilts in Westwood. He worked for me at Braverman-Mirisch as a copywriter while I was handling Raquel Welch, Barbara Parkins, and Barbara Eden. My office then was at 9200

Sunset Blvd. on the 4th floor. Ken remembers my dad had an office in our office that he came into every day. Ken also attended my mother's funeral; my mother committed suicide by hanging herself in her Beverly Hills home in 1966. It was the worst tragedy in my life and luckily, I remember very little of it.

Cynthia Ann Greene

In July, shortly after my mother died, Cynthia was a very innocent 19-year-old girl who lived in Brea and worked at Disneyland, where she won a Miss Photogenic contest. She came into my Sunset Boulevard office. I put a magazine cover in front of her and said can you pose like this? I told her she should be seen at a lot of Hollywood parties, like a big party put on by A&M Records, who was one of my clients at the time. I took her to the Luau in Beverly Hills.;I was also handling Anjanette Comer at the time. I took Cynthia to the premiere of *Hawaii*. In August I drove to her father's house in Brea in my bright red Chevrolet convertible. Her father was totally against my dating her, as I was Jewish and had a child. I eventually asked her to leave and I would get her a place to live in. She decided to leave home and moved into the Hilts House with Angela, Ruby, and myself. Angela actually called her Mom before we were even engaged.

On October 2, 1966, we got married in the living room of the house on Hilts. We had our honeymoon at The Arrowhead Inn in Lake Arrowhead. We had lots of parties at the Westwood house where I sometimes brought in a dance floor to celebrate 3 birthdays within one week: = me, Angela, and Cynthia. Cynthia remembers that we had British singing star Petula Clark and basketball legend Wilt Chamberlain over for dinner, plus other celebrities. We travelled to Mexico, Hawaii, London, Jamaica, Puerto Rico, and The Dominican Republic.

1967

I did some PR for a young singer by the name of Jesse Davis. He was performing at The Howard Manor Hotel, which was an "in spot" in those days in Palm Springs. He had been with a touring show band called *The Fabulous Tones*. I did publicity for him for a couple of years when he went out on his own. Fifty years later we got together on May 4, 2011, where I saw him perform at Humphrey's By The Bay, in downtown San Diego.

Now the new dimension: The 5th Dimension

Ron Townson, a member of a recording group who used to bartend at my parties, came up to me one day and said "Can you do PR for us?" I said "Do you have a record," and he said "No." I told him when they get one, call me. Shortly after that he called me and said we have one. It is Called "Up, Up and Away," which went on to become the number one single in the world. That year the group won five Grammy's. One day, Florence LaRue, of the group, came to me and said Marc Gordon, the manager of the group, and I want to get married, but we want to do something different. So, I then pulled off my second biggest stunt as a PR person (The other being Gary Lewis' last kiss on *The Ed Sullivan Show*).

The writer for their hit single was Jimmy Webb. Jimmy's father was an ordained minister, so, on a Sunday morning I took over the parking lot of The Century Plaza Hotel. We had chairs all set up in nice rows and 100 feet in the sky, in a balloon, Florence and Marc were married by Jimmy's father over a PA system that went directly to the ground so that all of the guests could hear the wedding vows. That Associated Press photo appeared the next day in EVERY paper in the world. We also made a trip to the White House and I have a photograph of myself with the group and their band on the lawn of the White House.

My son Michael was born on May 16, 1968 at 6:02 PM at Cedars of Lebanon Hospital on Fountain Avenue. His birth certificate said his name was David Michael Mirisch. It wasn't until April 15, 1974 that his name was legally changed to Michael David Mirisch. No idea how that happened at his birth. I'm sure it was a clerical error. It was also the year I handled my first PR client at the firm of Braverman and Mirisch. My partner was a dynamic and wonderful woman by the name of Millicent Braverman. We had an advertising and public relations agency. Millie handled the advertising accounts and I handled the PR. My uncles were nice enough to give us the Los Angeles United Artists radio and television campaigns for movies opening in LA. Millie also started handling the advertising for RB Furniture, with their first store, which eventually grew to 15 stores.

I was handling 15-20 clients at that time, mainly recording artists like Herb Alpert and The Tijuana Brass, Sergio Mendes and Brazil 66 (Mas Que Nada), Thelma Houston, Vic Dana (Red Roses for a Blue Lady), Nino and April (Deep Purple), Gale Garnett (We'll Sing in The Sunshine), The Edwin Hawkins Singers, The Dells (Oh What A Night), Dick Dale and The Del-Tones (Let's Go Trippin), Jackie DeShannon (Lonely Girl), Edwin Hawkins Singers (Oh Happy Day), and Gary Puckett (Young Girl and Woman Woman). My first real PR client was an actress by the name of Karen Steele. She was in her mid-twenties when I was handling her. She started her film career as a featured player in the Academy Award winning film, *Marty*, with Ernest Borgnine. She did over 75 feature films and I still have her headshots in my files. She died in 1988.

Farrah Fawcett

1968 was the year that I discovered a young lady who turned out to be America's number one poster girl in the 70's, Farrah Fawcett. I was handling publicity for some of Hollywood's most beautiful women at the time – Raquel Welch, Barbara Parkins of *Peyton Place*, Barbara Eden of *I Dream of Jeanie*, Lynda Carter of *Wonder Woman*, and Lindsay Wagner of *The Bionic Woman*.

The University of Texas was having a contest to find the "most beautiful girl on campus." They sent me pictures of 25 of the prettiest girls on campus. They said to pick one. I did, and it was Farrah. Even though all of the girls were "Texas beauties," there was something about Farrah that stood out, even then. I have always been asked on the television interviews that I have done through the years, "What was it?" I guess being from the midwest I liked the "All-American Girl" look, and that she had. I immediately called the university and said could you put me in touch with her parents. They did, but it took a year before I could convince them to bring her to Hollywood. She left school after her junior year and her mother drove her up to Los Angeles. I checked her into what was then called The Hollywood Studio Club — many of Hollywood's brightest young stars stayed there in the 40's, 50's, 60's, and 70's. During the first few months I got her picture in *The Los Angeles Times* for being Miss Boat Show and Miss Tennis Show. I also got her an appearance on *The Dating Game*.

I had my office then at 9200 Sunset Blvd. on the fourth floor. A few floors above us was one of the top theatrical agencies at the time, IFA. One of the agents was my good friend, Dick Clayton. I took her up to meet him, and right there on the spot he signed her to be an IFA client. Shortly after that he took her to Screen Gems (Columbia Pictures) and they signed her to a contract. Lee Majors was also a client of Dick's, and through that introduction, Farrah and Lee start-ing going to all kinds of Hollywood social functions.

I don't remember much from that period, and there really isn't anyone today that I can talk to about it. I know we did some publicity things and six months later I get a letter from a lawyer (that I still have in my file), thanking me for my work on behalf of Farrah, and here is a commission check for $200. Of all of the pictures I have taken with clients, Hollywood stars, and famous athletes, I never took a picture with Farrah. Back in those days, publicists didn't seem to do that. I still have all of the original pictures that Farrah's family sent me back then and I am sure a few will look good in my book. When Farrah passed away from cancer on June 25, 2009, I started to receive calls from all of the major networks. I guess most of the media looked up and found out that I discovered Farrah.

MSNBC was the first to call around 9:00 AM and had me live on a voice-over as they showed pictures. We were living at our condo in LaCosta at that time and ABC, NBC, and KTLA sent crews over to the house to do interviews with me at our condo pool. Just a few weeks before her death, *E* sent a camera crew and reporter down to interview me. They actually did not air it on the day of her death, but ran it as a special a few weeks later.

After Farrah left me she eventually signed with my fellow pub-licist and friend, Jay Bernstein. It took him eight years to get her *Charlie's Angels* and release the world-famous poster that had sold over 12,000,000 copies by her death. I have always felt that IF she had stayed with me things would have happened sooner, and that there were 8 years there that she could have developed much faster into the international star that she eventually became. But, that's looking back and it has never done me any good in my life to "look back at what could have been." I also stated in my various interviews through the years if I had not discovered Farrah, the odds would have been that she would have graduated college and married her college sweetheart, Greg Lott, and lived happily ever after on a big Texas ranch.

May she rest in peace.

Wilt Chamberlain

This was also the year the great "Wilt the Stilt" Chamberlain was traded to the Los Angeles Lakers from the Philadelphia 76er's. Everyone in the world knew Wilt, and his arrival in Los Angeles was a major happening. He was black and 7'2". Somehow, I was referred to him and he hired me to throw a series of parties for him at this majestic big home he custom built at the top of Mulholland Drive. He had it built for a man of his size. He called it "Ursa Major." He had four big Great Danes that were the love of his life.

The first party I organized was his "House Warming." Everyone in town had heard about this incredible home he had built. He had a pool in his living room that opened up to the outside of his house. Above his triple king-sized bed he had a skylight that would open when he pushed a button. He could also lie in his bed and push a button and the curtains would open up. For that first party, during the day we had all of his business friends come over and we had a string quartet playing. About 6:00, when this group left, we got ready for the younger crowd with a rock and roll band. Two different parties, two different crowds, two different menus.

From then on I organized dinner parties every week, of a dozen or so people who sat around a big round dinner table fit for a king. I also organized many parties where Wilt and I would invite 25 girls and a bunch of his male friends. The girls would come to the gate with their boyfriends and the security guards would turn the guys away as their names were not on the list. One of downstairs rooms was a total waterbed.

Whenever you would pass by that room and see Wilt's shoes and a pair of tiny shoes outside the door, you knew he was having a good old time with one of the 20,000 women that he said he went to bed with (as documented in his autobiography). I was in charge of all of the parties, from working with caterers, getting the bartenders, ordering security, and valet. Many of the pictures in his book on the house that was eventually printed were stars that I invited to attend his parties.

Encino Tennis Court Home

IN 1970 I bought the Encino home with the tennis court, the pool, and the cabana guesthouse. I only owed $10,000 on the Hilts house at that time. Cynthia's sister Fran lived with us in the Hilts house and moved to Encino in the guesthouse with us for a little while. People we had come over for dinner were Perry Como and Wilt Chamberlain. We had lots of celebrities come to our house to play tennis there – William Shatner (who was not very well known then), Richard Crenna, Jane Alexander, and Lyle Waggoner. Cynthia said we used to have over 50-100 people every weekend. We had tournaments once a month when everyone came over. I really loved that house and hated to give it up when we had to sell it. When we sold it we lost $90,000 on it, which is the reason my father disinherited me. Whenever he wanted to take Angela out on a weekend he would drive to the base of our home on High Valley Place and wait for me to bring her down the driveway. The home had movie stars and producers living on all sides of us.

Elvis Presley and Perry Como

1970. Cynthia remembers the evening we were at The International Hotel with Elvis and Priscilla Presley. We went to see his show with Frank Lieberman of the *Los Angeles Herald Examiner*. In 1962 Elvis starred in two films for The Mirisch Corporation – *Kid Galahad* and *Follow That Dream,* so he knew my name. We were in Las Vegas for Elvis' closing night and Perry Como's Opening Night.

Perry Como,
David Mirisch

Perry was making his first nightclub appearance in 20 years and he hired me to handle the publicity for his engagement. One of things I remember is a person came up to his top floor suite to do an interview. The first question he asked Perry was, "What was your first record?" As a good PR man I said to him "Have you read Perry's bio?" He said that no, he had not. I said to him, "Here is Perry's bio. Go sit outside and when you have read it let me know and we'll start the interview over again." During my PR career I was always a big one for detailed and accurate bios. I felt if I provided the press and media with all of the "facts," the time could be well spent on having a great interview.

Irving Mirisch

My father died of a heart attack in 1971. He and his wife, Dorothy, and another couple were on their way from the Shubert Theatre when he had a heart attack in the car. His funeral was held on March 15 at Hillside Memorial Park, and Dr. Max Nussbaum delivered the eulogy. My father was a very sincere man, utterly honest; a man of integrity and a big heart. He loved life and liked people. Through the years, he donated money to The Jewish Home for the Aged, The Guardians, and United Jewish Appeal. At the time of his death he and his second wife, Dorothy, lived on Beverly Glen. I vaguely remember going to their apartment in grief and Dorothy did not console me one bit. I later found out that when she died, all of my father's paintings and possessions were given to her daughter Sandy. Nothing to my sister or myself.

Cynthia and I moved into a bungalow at the Ambassador Hotel for a few months. I handled publicity at the Cocoanut Grove, and for a number of the headliners who performed there: Don Ho, Dick Jensen, Eddy Arnold, Tom Jones, Petula Clark, Mrs. Miller, Deacon Jones, Rosey Grier. I'll never forget one night I was standing at the entrance to The Cocoanut Grove Ballroom in my tuxedo, greeting the stars as they came in. A man came up to me and thought I was a maître d'hotel and handed me a $50 bill and said, "Can you get us a good table?" I kept the $50 and got him his table.

We moved into The Marina City Club and lived on the Promenade. We opened our doors and the water and the yachts were right in front of us. Cynthia, Michael, Angela, and I lived there. Michael must have been about 5 years old when he did something that caused a lot of anxiety with Cynthia and I. He went up to the top of the building and was walking around the top floor. He thought it was "cool" when he looked down and saw fire engines all over the place coming to rescue him.

Cynthia and I got divorced in 1973. I moved into an apartment in West Hollywood right near Santa Monica Blvd. and East of La Cienega. I lived there for about a year. The only thing I really remember about it was that I cooked a lot of cube steaks, as that was all I knew how to cook.

I had two life-threatening incidents. The first happened in Palm Springs. I used to take Michael and his adopted brother, Carlos, down to the desert and we stayed at the home of one of my first clients, Trini Lopez, who I had met when he was performing at PJ's on Santa Monica Blvd. in West Hollywood. Trini came on the music scene very quickly with two number one hits: "If I Had a Hammer" and "LaBamba." The boys used to climb the very steep hills, and on one particular weekend I decided to join them. I had a date with me and we started to walk up the incline. The boys almost got to the top when all of a sudden I took a spill. Instead of walking as I should have, I was taking big steps. Well, I missed a rock and all of a sudden started rolling down the hill that had lots of boulders on it. As I was tossing and turning, the first thing that popped into my mind was the story of the snow ski racer Jill Kinmont who fell during a race, broke her back and was paralyzed. In that flash of a second I said "Dear Lord, don't let this happen to me." As active as I was I just couldn't stand the thought of being in a wheelchair the rest of my life.

One of the neighbors down below heard my incredibly loud screams and called 911. The boys started hearing fire engines headed in my direction and saw that my car was still at the foot of the hill. It took them an hour to get to the top and 20 minutes to get down. When they got where I was, the paramedics had already put me on a gurney and we were headed to the closest hospital. They said I might have a broken vertebrae or back. But, God was looking out over me, as he has throughout my life and there was no serious injury. Michael remembers that I was taken back to the house on Federal Avenue and was in bed working from home for a good two months. He said I had a real difficult time in moving at all.

The second incident I don't remember at all, but Michael seems to remember it pretty vividly. We were with some friends and were hiking in the hills near Griffith Park. Michael said he slipped off the side of a cliff and I went to grab him and he pulled me down with him. We were both hanging on by a limb until someone came and rescued the two of us. To this day, he said I saved his life.

1978 – David Sidell

1978 was when I began my friendship with David Sidell. He owned a chain of restaurants called Josephina's, and then opened a few called The Bratskellar. One of those was located right on the corner of Westwood Boulevard, just one block north of Wilshire Blvd. That year I formed The Josephina's Celebrity Basketball Team. We had regular uniforms and warm-ups. Character actor Ron Masak and the catcher for the Los Angeles Dodgers, Steve Yeager, helped me put the team together. I had all of the stars of the Dodgers playing on our team – Steve Garvey, Ron Cey, Tommy John, Rick Rhoden, future Hall of Famer Don Sutton, Jimmy "The Toy Cannon" Wynn, Davey Lopes, Mark Cresse, Reggie Smith, and Glenn Burke. The Dodgers had just played in the World Series that year, so the timing was perfect. We played 21 games against high school faculties. Once I put the word out, our schedule was complete in a few days. Our record was 19-2 and both games we lost at the buzzer. We played to capacity crowds. I rented a motor home and usually one of the guys would drive.

One game I accepted was at the China Lake Air Naval Weapons

Station. I didn't check where it was and when we got in the motor home we found it was 150 miles northeast of Los Angeles, out near the Mojave Desert. That was the last time I ever booked a game not knowing where it was. David Sidell and I did lots of things together in the next few years. I put on parties for him at his various restaurants in Westwood, Sherman Oaks, Palm Springs, Century City, and even one at The Bratskellar in La Jolla, where we honored jockeys Willie Shoemaker and Willie Hartack (and Wilt Chamberlain showed up for that too). We threw a party at The Marina Del Rey Brakskellar for sickle cell anemia, and Wilt and Lakers teammates Happy Hairston and Jim McMillan showed up.

David remembers me setting singers like Glen Campbell and Linda Ronstadt to sing the National Anthem at Dodgers games. In fact, I think this was the year I booked most of the Anthem singers, and in return received four season tickets. David attended a number of Victor Awards as my guest and went on a number of tennis tournaments with me to Guadalajara, Palm Desert, and Phoenix. Some of the celebrities who played in all of my tournaments at that time were Lyle Waggoner (*Wonder Woman* and *The Carol Burnett Show*), Dick Van Patten (*Eight Is Enough*), Ben Murphy (*Alias Smith and Jones*), and Peter Brown (*Lawman*). He remembers going backstage with me at The Cocoanut Grove at the old Ambassador Hotel to meet Sonny and Cher, at The Greek Theatre to meet Johnny Mathis, and at the Las Vegas Hilton to meet Liberace. (I have pictures with all of these stars).

He also remembers us playing at Dr.Mark Saginor's house in Beverly Hills with Johnny Carson, Ross Martin, Willie Shoemaker, Dan Rowan (*Laugh-In*), and Carroll Rosenbloom and Ed Hookstratton from The Los Angeles Rams. We were always joined by our good friends Paul Bloch (Rogers & Cowan PR) and Richard Berger, who went on to become a top executive at 20th Century Fox and Walt Disney Studios. Rick was one of the nicest guys you could ever meet. He passed away in 2007. David also remembers that I fixed him up on a few dates with Cheryl Miller (*Daktari*). I've always said that no one could ever say a bad thing about my good friend David Sidell.

I put The Los Angeles Aztec soccer cheerleading team together in 1979. The team was a member of the North American Soccer League. Three of the girls from the Rams squad joined me (Cindy Landis, Susan James, and Michelle Kotzen). That was the first time I met Rhonda Shear who, for 7 years, hosted the USA cable show *Up All Night*. I managed this squad for two years and they played their games at the Rose Bowl. Unlike the Rams squad, we added four guys to this team. The second year a few more of the girls from the Rams squad joined us. I guess they weren't too happy that Rams management was doing things the way they did.

Trip to China to Film a TV Special

March 8, 1982 — of all the travelling that I have done in my life, this experience has to be a highlight. While I was in Portland, Oregon for one of my events, I met a young producer by the name of Charles Jennings who was associated with World Pacific Pictures. He had formed a company to produce a television special called *Cycling Through China*. He hired me to book the stars, promote the bicycles, hire a makeup-hair-stylist, and see to a lot of the personal things we would need for the trip, like helmets, gloves, and trail mix (my idea). We were going to travel from Hong Kong/Macau in southeastern China, to Canton. We rode our bikes 20-25 miles per day. You could ride as much as you wanted to. When you got tired they put your bike in the van and you rode on the bus. I was able to line up to join us, Lorne Greene (*Bonanza*),

Kate Jackson (*Charlie's Angels*) Ben Vereen (nightclub and Broadway star), Joe Cunningham (Harlem Globetrotters), Lindsay Bloom (a former Miss USA), Brandon Scott (magician), Paul Horn (flutist), Mark Wenzel (mime), and Mayf Nutter (country-western entertainer). Charles was also able to get prizewinning internationally recognized *TIME Magazine* photographer, David Hume Kennerly to join us.

We were under the supervision of the Chinese government as we were going into communes that had not seen many white people before, and probably had never seen black people before. Ben and Joe were a big hit as Joe carried a Polaroid camera and took pictures of the people and instantly gave them a picture – the likes of what they had never seen before. Ben used his video camera and played back what he took of the people. This totally amazed them. All of us bicycled as much as we could each day. I would get my usual leg cramps and would have to take a break. So, the leg cramps that started in high school tennis followed me through China and to present day living.

David Mirisch China

David Mirisch China

One fun experience was one day, while I was riding around a city, I came upon a girls' basketball team and I shot some hoops with them. On one of our rides I hit a mean bump in the road and my camera bag flew out of the basket and my camera landed on the pavement. Something with the lens was broken, thus the camera being totally useless. There I was, in the middle of communist China, and no one to fix my camera, which was the most important part of my trip – to take good pictures to show my friends and family back home. I thought I had taken my last picture until David gave me an extra one he had. A nice gesture by a nice man. Thanks to David Hume Kennerly — he came to my rescue when I needed him.

Kate Jackson joined us halfway through the trip. She brought along her secretary, hairdresser, and manager, Bill Samath, who used to work for me when I was a partner with Shelly Saltman. I had given him his first job in the entertainment business. On March 22, we finally made it to Canton, our final destination. We had a nice hotel and the first thing I ordered were two cheeseburgers and a chocolate Sunday. I didn't do really well on the food during the trip, due to my Midwest meat and potatoes upbringing. Thanks to the trail mix, Hershey kisses, and a big jar of peanut butter I brought on the trip, I was always able to fill my stomach. They served lots of "greens," which many times looked like they floated out of my garden. They brought whole pigs and large fish to the tables that were passed around like at a U.S. Chinese restaurant, and you took off as much as you wanted. I always asked for rolls or bread for my peanut butter, and an orange soda.

Lorne Greene joined us in Canton as he was going to be the American co-host of our big show that we were going to do in Main Square of the city. We spent three days touring the area and getting some beautiful scenic shots of the countryside and the waterfalls. I took Lorne Greene to the office of the mayor of Canton and he presented him a proclamation from Los Angeles Mayor, Tom Bradley. We then went to the Sun Yat Sen Memorial Center where Lorne taped his interview for *Entertainment Tonight*.

March 28 was the day we were going to tape the big show. When we got to the Center at 8:30 AM it was raining, but by 1:00 pm the sun was shining and we started to shoot the performance. Everyone in the group did something and we felt the thousands of Chinese in attendance enjoyed it. Lorne had a popular local television personality as his host, so everyone in the audience knew what we were doing. My general overall observations of China at that time: the hustle and bustle of city life and bicycles everywhere and people working the fields with water buffalo like they have been doing for generations; this was their version of a modern-day tractor. Their countryside's had some of the most beautiful scenery in the world. People were friendly. They looked at us with curiosity but treated you with respect. They always tried to speak a little English, even if it was just a few words. Many of the people lived on what they grew in their communes. They never made it into the bigger cities. They lived and died were they were born and grew up in.

Family was the most important thing to them. Their meals consisted of rice, fish, pork, chicken, eggs, vegetables, and tiny spare ribs. They drank a lot of tea and coffee. We had no milk or dairy products, ice cream, salads, or real beef anywhere along our route. The people had never seen bicycles with gears, so everywhere we went we drew crowds of interest. One day when I was shopping by myself, 50 people followed me to a store to look at my bike when I went inside. Most villagers knew how to say "hello" and "good-bye," and those were the only words of English they knew. But, they would try and practice their English with you. It made us feel good to hear those words coming from them to us. All in all, it was an "experience of a lifetime." When, I look back on this trip I'm sorry I didn't know Sandy at this time, as we would both would have been able to share this memory forever. It didn't work out that way, so I'll share this one with my readers.

Current Wife —
My Best Friend and Love of My Life — Sandy Mirisch
Summer of 1982 — **this** was the year I remet Sandy and my daughter to be, Summer. I had worked with Sandy 15 years ago when she was an agent with her mother at The Toni Kelman Agency. They were one of the two top theatrical agencies for children. They had handled the careers of most of *The Brady Bunch*, Willie Aames of *Eight is Enough*, Lance Kerwin of *James at 15*, and future Academy Award winning actress Jodie Foster, from the ages of 4 through14 years old.

One day I called Toni just to check in and I said "Where was Sandy?" She said she and Summer were living in Hemet. I told her the next day I had to drive to Palm Springs for a meeting and would call Sandy.

Sandy and Summer met me at a Denny's restaurant in Beaumont, right at the intersection of highways 10 and 60. I was driving a red convertible at the time. I had been at Disneyland the night before and picked up some presents for Summer, who was three at the time. That did it.

Right then and there she took to me. I made a number of trips to Hemet to take Sandy out, and after six of them I said "I can't make this drive anymore." We had gotten very romantic and I said if you want to see me anymore you and Summer need to move into my house on Federal Avenue in West Los Angeles. I had a nice home and there was an extra room for the two of them. I said, give it a try. If you don't like it, you can always move home. She kept her home in Hemet "just in case," but eventually moved in lock, stock, and barrel.

Year of 1985

My wonderful Sandy threw me a great 50th party at Flakey Jake's restaurant, located at the intersection of Pico and Sepulveda Boulevards in West Los Angeles. It was one of my clients at the time so they took care of the food and beverages. We had a small singing group entertain. Sandy had gotten stand-up wall sections and put up pictures of me from a baby until that year. In attendance were many of my actor friends and athletes like Wilt Chamberlain, Elgin Baylor, and Olympic gold medal skier, Bill Johnson. (I have a picture in my 70th birthday party book of Sandy, I, Wilt, and Dick Janik).

1991 – Sandy and I moved into my dream home located on the 4th green of the south course at LaCosta Country Club in North County San Diego. The front side of our house faced LaCosta Avenue so we were one of only three houses that faced both the course and the street. We had been living in our nice house on Federal Avenue when my former partner, Steve Simons, called me and said you have to move down here to LaCosta. I told him it wouldn't work for me as I felt I had to be in the heart of things in Beverly Hills, close to my Hollywood connections. But, I had Sandy go down and she started looking around. So, we eventually picked up our things and Sandy, Summer, and I moved into what Michael called "Camp David."

I still have lots of pictures in my files. It was 4,500 square feet – three levels, once owned by Jenny Craig. The bottom level had a big poolroom, bar, and walk in wine cellar. The second floor was the dining room, kitchen, breakfast area, master bedroom, and two guest rooms. The third floor was a lounging area with a giant TV screen. I eventually put my intern up here. There was a big cement wall separating the driveway and the house. In between was a nice grass area where I put my giant white horse statue, and what had been a guesthouse I turned into my office. In the backyard we had a big pool and a nice Jacuzzi. There were also steps down to the golf cart path so at the end of a day we could practice putting, as the green was right opposite our house.

We used to entertain a lot. Michael and Angela and friends and family would come down on weekends and we had great parties at the pool and in the billiard room and bar. We had two big couches that four people could sleep on. Every year for ten years we had our "Oscar Party." It was always the talk of La Costa. We had at least 50 people and printed out ballots where we had a contest to see who could guess the most winners. We always gave a fun prize to the winner. We had TV sets on in all the rooms. People were comfortably spread out from one floor to another. We did a "pot-luck" so we had all kinds of foods and beverages.

Talking about beverages, one of things I will never forget is when we went to move out to our new place in Encinitas I lifted up the floorboards in the wine cellar, and, low and behold, I found about 50 empty mini bottles of vodka and whiskeys. Since Sandy and I always were flown first class we always asked for extra bottles and brought them home. Since there were so many I never kept track of them. One day I asked Summer where they were and she finally confessed when we were away they used to have parties at the house and were consuming all of our mini bottles and throwing them under the wood planks, as she knew we would never lift them while we were living there. With our approval, she put in some stone steps on the east side of the house and painted one with her name on it. just as she did (which we didn't know about) in the rear of her closet. When local NFL retired player Pete Shaw moved into our house with a roommate a year or so after we moved out, he found Summer's name there and mentioned it to me at one of our golf tournaments.

Year of 1995

The family all got together at the Beverly Hills Country Club on Motor Avenue, where my family had been members when we lived in Los Angeles before. Everyone was there, but of course my mom and dad and Harold and Lottie. Otherwise, every son, daughter, and cousin was in the group picture (I have on our wall) except my lover-boy son, Michael. He was picking up a girl at the airport and instead of him being there for the picture she wanted to go home and change. He should have just been firm and said "You look fine, we have to be on time." But, he gave in to her and missed being in the picture.

U.S.S. Midway Aircraft Carrier

This was also the year that I became a member of The Board of Directors for the U.S.S. Midway Aircraft Carrier Museum. It was active for 47 years and was the longest serving U.S. Navy carrier in the 20th century, and the largest ship in the world between 1945-1955. Since it docked in San Diego in 2004 it has become the most visited floating ship museum in the World. A Del Mar businessman by the name of Alan Uke had a vision to take this great carrier out of mothballs in Bremerton, Washington and bring it to San Diego and make it a museum. The San Diego Convention and Visitors Bureau always said the most asked question by tourists is "can we visit a ship?" After, 9-11 that was not allowed anymore.

I read in the paper of Alan's dream, and since my uncles had produced the movie *Midway*, with Charlton Heston, Hal Holbrook, and Henry Fonda, I thought it would be a natural to offer my services to be part of the organizing team. I was on the board of directors for eight years, and about 20 of us met once a month. I was able to make two important contributions. The first was I brought down my longtime friend, comedian Buddy Hackett, for a lunch on board the ship with potential donors. They gave him a Midway cap and he was a big hit (I have some pictures in my Midway notebook). Secondly, I brought down another actor friend, Cliff Robertson, who starred in many feature films, such as *Charly*, for which he won the Oscar for best performance by an actor. He also played John F. Kennedy in the Navy war movie *PT 109*, and starred opposite the beautiful Kim Kovak in one of my favorite films, *Picnic*. Since Cliff was from nearby La Jolla, and he had a house here, he was willing to come down and do some interviews and narrate a promotional film.

When the carrier was ready to leave North Island there were about 1,000 of us invited to make the voyage across the harbor where it would be docked permanently. My son Michael joined Sandy and I, and he and I even made it up the captain's nest and took a few pictures there. On June 5, 2004, Walter Mirisch was invited down to help officially "open the Midway" to the public. All of his family came down and we have a great picture of all of us standing in front of a fighter plane on the upper deck of this great ship. It was a moment all of us in the Mirisch family were very proud of.

Carlsbad Fires

1996, October 10 — this day was one of the most "frightening" days of our married life. It was the day the Carlsbad fires took place. There were fires all over the area. They were even threatening La Costa Canyon High School. Firetrucks were at the top of LaCosta Avenue just in case the fires would start to come up our street. To the North we could see fires starting to come through the canyons headed directly towards the La Costa Golf Course. If it got that far, with all of the trees lining the fairways of the golf course, it would have run right up to our home. Michael saw it on television, and being the great son that he is, he got 3-4 of his best friends who had 4-wheel drive SUV's and immediately headed towards "Camp David."

Sandy, Summer, and I started to load our three cars with photo albums, pictures, computers, and especially my sports scrapbooks. We didn't even think about clothes, as those we could always buy. So, once Michael got to the house we stood at the edge of the pool watching the flames slowly work their way down the canyon. Then, an act of God (for us at least) happened. When the fire got to near Alga Street, just a few blocks away, the winds shifted due west. Unfortunately, there was an entire block or two of homes that were burned to the ground. Our prayers were answered and our beautiful home was saved.

Pancreatic Cancer

In 1997 I met a lady by the name of Pamela Marquardt. She found me somehow and said she wanted to start a non-profit to start helping people with pancreatic cancer. She said I didn't take her seriously at first, but told her I would do what I could to help her. So, she gathered 22 of her family and friends that had all been touched in one way or another. Stephanie Davis became the chairperson. We met every few weeks and did our first event at the Beverly Hills Hotel with 250 people. The next year went to The Beverly Hilton Hotel for 500 people, and the next year we went to the Universal Hilton Hotel for 1,000 people. The first year we honored the late Michael Landon of *Bonanza* that died of pancreatic cancer. The next year we honored the great musical writer Henry Mancini that had also died of pancreatic cancer. Thus, The Pancreatic Cancer Action Network was born, which is now international. In 2010 they did their annual Gala that raised over $800,000. They now do over 75 events a year throughout the United States.

David's 70Th Birthday Party

My beautiful Sandy put on a great 70th birthday party for me at the Calabasas Country Club in the San Fernando Valley in July 2005. We had about 100 people. Uncle Walter even showed up with his son Andrew. Many of my former clients were there, including my real early ones like Anjanette Comer and Maggie Blye. In attendance were people like my former lawyer Michael Harris, Barbara Luna, Robert and Gwynne Pine, Mitzi McCall and Charlie Brill, Bruce Belland, Omar and Veronica Veytia from Tijuana, Alan Thicke, Joseph Mascolo, Caryn Richman, Wayne Orkin, Stella Stevens, Kari Michaelsen, Dick Janik, Florence LaRue, E.J.Peaker, Roman Salicki, and David Sidell.

My friend Irwin "Jake" Shorr came in from his home in Maryland and brought with him 7 incredible gifts. He had sent letters out to famous athletes asking them to sign something personal to me. The ones he got read "Happy 70th Birthday to David Mirisch." He got a picture signed by former heavyweight boxing champion Joe Frazier, and balls signed by Hall of Famers New York Yankee Yogi Berra, San Francisco 49ers quarterback, Joe Montana, and former Los Angeles Lakers great, Jerry West.

My longtime friend and poet, Bruce Sievers, wrote a poem about me and read it, as did my sister Nan. Bruce Belland of *The Four Preps* wrote a song about me and sang it to the crowd. The day was only spoiled (probably only in my eyes) by my wonderful granddaughter Chloe, who was about three at the time. When I went to go on stage and give my speech, which meant a great deal to me, Chloe was running up on the back of the stage and in front of the stage distracting everyone. I didn't stop my speech to ask Michael or Vicky to stop what she was doing, as I thought that they would. They never did. When I asked Michael about it later he just said, "She was a little girl and just having fun." I think that incident will be one of those things that I will never forget. I always wished I could have started over.

The Kentucky Derby

May 2009 I experienced a "bucket list" item. Sandy and I attended the Kentucky Derby. We were hired by a Tonya York Dees to bring some Hollywood celebrities down. Part of my deal was two first class tickets, a suite at the Gault Hotel, and two VIP tickets to the gala put on by the James Graham Brown Cancer Center. We brought down Marg Helgenberger from the television series "CSI" and actress Valerie Bertinelli. We took some nice pictures at the gala, which we ended up using for our 2009 Christmas card.

We went to the Oaks Races on Friday and the Derby on Saturday. The most fun part of the trip was when Sandy, Valerie, her boyfriendg Tom Vitaleg and I were driven to Churchill Downs. We had a police sergeant as our driver and we did not make one stop from the time we left the Gault Hotel until we pulled up at the front gate at Churchill Downs. On the Debry race, I picked 10 horses at $2.00 each. Of them, one happened to win. He was a 50-1 long shot so I ended up winning $100.00. It was a fun experience but I don't have a desire to go back again. It was a great experience but I can say, "I was there."

David Mirisch Lifetime Achievement Award
November 8 – this was possibly the proudest moment of my life. I had been on the board of directors for 8 years of a non-profit called Photocharity. A great guy created it by the name of Jeffrey Sitcov. He had been a photographer and to this day I still don't know how he supports himself. I never asked. Didn't think it was my business. One day, he said to himself, I want to create a non-profit to help people. He wasn't sure who this was going to be, but one day he heard the story of The Storefront. It is a shelter in the downtown district of San Diego called Hillcrest. There were over 2,000 teenagers a night sleeping on the streets, every night. This shelter provides lodging for teens that are willing to get off the street and try and get back to a normal way of living. These were teens that were thrown out of their homes by their parents or who had gone from foster home to foster home. Some became prostitutes. Many were on drugs and alcohol. We started to do one concert a year to raise money to help build educational and musical programs for them. We even formed a band called the *TNT Band*.We did concerts at Humphrey's and Anthology, and dinners at the Lomas Santa Fe Country Club. We had acts like Eve Selis and AJ Croce donate their time. One year we even rented out San Diego State Stadium and hired BB King to headline our show. Through the 8 years I never personally got any direct cash donations, but I "mentored" Jeffrey and gave him many ideas of what to do and not to do.

In our first 8 years, we raised over $1,500,000. So, on Sunday night, November 8, 2009, Photocharity established "The David Mirisch Mentorship Angel Award." It will be given each year to a person in San Diego County that "helps homeless teenagers."

We had 250 people in the audience. Summer flew in from Montana, Angela took the train down from Lompoc, and Michael and Vicky drove down from Encino. Our good friend Jennifer Josephs flew in from Salt Lake City, my cousin Carol Mirisch was there, as she had recently moved to Solana Beach, and my longtime friend, Irwin "Jake" Shorr, was visiting his family in Los Angeles and he drove down too. I knew I was being honored, but there were a few surprises. When I was being introduced they flashed pictures on the giant video screen of myself with major stars from my past. And, they also ran these pictures in the centerfold of the program. And, even on the back cover, two of the homeless teenagers from The Storefront wrote personal thank you's to me.

I had taken careful time to write my acceptance speech, as I wanted it to say what I have done and felt in doing over 2,500 fundraising events for every kind of cause you can think of. In my 40 years in the business, this was the greatest honor I had ever received: a lifetime achievement award in my name. It will be a moment I will never forget. When my two-minute speech was over I brought up Sandy and my three kids. I thought I was going to break down and start crying, but I stayed strong and just showed my appreciation to the audience and how proud of a moment it was for me.

December 25 (Christmas Day) – For the first time in my life I did not spend Christmas morning with any of my kids and grandchildren. Sandy and I decided to give something back for the good life we have been blessed with. We went to downtown San Diego and helped serve over 2,000 homeless, hungry, and needy people their Christmas Day dinner. First, Sandy and I helped stuff over 1,000 bags with apples, oranges, and wrapped muffins. Then, we helped escort people to their seats and then Sandy served people their dinners. While there I was introduced to the mayor of San Diego and we had a nice chat. Also, KUSI did an interview with me for the news that night. We had exchanged our Christmas presents the night before so we were more than happy to do what we did Christmas morning.

Interview with Jason Felts, CEO of Virgin Produced

How did you meet David?
My very first contact with David wasn't even in person. David was a guest speaker at my college in San Diego. I ended up missing the class and when I came back the next week I received the bad news that I missed the best guest speaker!

I started to question what I had missed, talking to students and faculty. I proceeded to approach my professor and begged him to set me up to meet with David. After missing the class, all I truly wanted to do was to meet David. The professor was a good friend of David's, and over the course of a week it was something I continued to be very persistent on, until I met "The" David.

And then you met David?
David invited me to his house at the golf course. I pulled into the gated home with two golden retrievers running out to greet me. I was told to wait in the courtyard. The anticipation of meeting David at this time was building. David opened the guesthouse door and told me to "Get in here." I was whisked into his office, which was in the guesthouse. On the walls were hundreds of pictures, old and new, of David with

celebrities. That was my very first encounter. We spoke briefly and I didn't just realize I wanted to meet David, but also wanted to work for him. At the end of our brief conversation I told David I would love to be his assistant.

Jason Felts and David Mirisch

David responded with "I don't hire men...well, because the last man I hired ended up with one of my female assistants and marrying her. I ended up losing them both."

By that point in time, during our conversation, I just couldn't take it anymore and offered to work for David for free for the first six months to prove myself. The word "free" resonated in David's ears.

I started working with David, helping with his events. Some David was at and some he wasn't. It was roughly 50 a year that David would attend.

There was a loft in the guesthouse on David's property and all I wanted to do was have his desk up there, overlooking the golf course. Roughly 3-6 months later David told me, "Lisa (his current assistant) is moving to LA," and he offered me the job as his permanent assistant. It was then I began to travel "the world of David" and learned a lot. It was a great foundation on learning to be held accountable and be proactive. Knowing everything before something hits the fan. David was a man who never said "No." It was something that was difficult to maintain as his assistant — That's because David was so proactive himself with everything he did. And it was a good thing!

Jason, I would like for you to tell me about working an event with David. The "in's and out's" of the journey David would take you through.

Let me tell you about the Victor Awards in Las Vegas. ...

The Victor Awards was the sports celebrity event of the year before ESPN was ever heard of. Sports and entertainment celebrities would gather to celebrate the year's favorite athletes. This was my very first event out of Los Angeles and first time in Vegas, at the Hilton Hotel, at the end of the strip where Elvis was a frequent performer. Sports legends attending were Yogi Berra, Shaquille O'Neal, and Joe Namath. It was everybody and anybody of the who's who.

Night one of the Victor awards I was told to assure all the celebrities got to their rooms correctly. I was given the headshots of each star, and as the limos pulled up I would escort them to check-in and then wherever they needed to go. After that I wouldn't see them until an hour before the event began.

I was assigned by David to take the stars out for a night on the town. I decided to order a limo from the reception desk, not knowing what I was doing. I joined the celebrities in the limo and we all headed to one of the hot Vegas nightclubs. A few hours went by and this pretty blonde haired girl came up to me and said, "There is a group of us ready to go home, can you call the limo to take us back." I did just that and as the limo pulled up she offered to take me with them. I thought about it for one moment, just one moment, and said "Okay." We got into the limo and back to the hotel. While in the limo a VIP afterparty was in the works.

My new, beautiful blonde friend decided to offer her room for the after party. As we got to the hotel front desk our friend realized she didn't have her key. The desk manager offered to give her another key provided she showed ID, which she did not have. The front desk said "Dear lady, I cannot provide you with a key if you have no ID. How do I even know you belong to this hotel?" "If you could please escort me to my room I have my ID in my bag up there." We all took the elevator to the Hilton Hotels Penthouse suite. The door was unlocked, she ran to her bed, picked up her wallet from her purse and showed the bell hop her ID, which simply said, as I looked at it myself, "Paris Hilton!" I was getting ready now for a memorable night.

Cut to the next morning, everyone is still in the room, no one has slept, my phone is ringing and ringing; it is David looking for me. I ran down to the lobby to meet him in a hurry.

David asked me where I was. "I was looking for you everywhere."

"I was in the penthouse suite with Paris Hilton and people.

David said, "Good Job! Go get ready and come back here."

I discovered right then and there that what I thought was going to be a bad situation with David was actually exactly what he wanted me to do; take care of the guests.

Do you still know Paris to this day?

Yes, I still know Paris very well!

Did anything ever go terribly wrong when working that had to be solved quickly?

I can't really think of anything...nothing, at least, that couldn't be solved. There was one time; it was a golf tournament event with Lou Rawls ("You'll Never Find Another Love Like Mine"). I actually had no idea who he was and had to call my dad and ask him. I was with him on the golf course; we were having a great time, getting loud and rowdy. When the tournament was over and everyone was heading back to his or her room to get ready for the evening festivities to begin, Lou said, "you know I don't think I can sing tonight." His voice was shot from the daytime events. I had to go tell David. I went up to his room and knocked on the door and no one answered. I just kept knocking and knocking. David never naps, he's like a vampire, but in this case from all the hooting and hollering on the golf course, he was napping. When he finally answered the door, I said, "Lou doesn't think he can sing tonight, he doesn't really have a voice anymore from this afternoon."

David walked over to the desk in his room and picked up one of those hotel note pads and started writing a bunch of stuff down, like a prescription. Came back over to me, rips the page off the pad and told me to go get this stuff; two lemons, honey, hot water, all the things he needs, and to bring it back to him. There was a Denny's next door from the hotel and I got all the stuff from there and I brought it back to David. David starts preparing this hot tea and took it down to Lou himself. Lou drank it and an hour later, Bam!, Lou's performing.

Out of all the stars you met with David, whom were you really impressed with?

I am actually more "star struck" about world leaders and politicians, not so much celebrities. BUT, if I had to pick someone, it would be meeting Yogi Berra. I grew up watching baseball with my family. One event I was told by David that I was going to have to pick Yogi and his wife up at the airport because the original driver got sick. I was scared out of my mind driving this big communal van. I got to the airport, set the back of the bus up nice with something to drink, got myself out of the van, and held up a sign with his name on it and waited his arrival.

While I was waiting, I kept asking passengers if they had seen Yogi on the plane. It seems Yogi spoke with all of them. Finally, he came out. When we found each other, we said hello, I started to put the luggage on the bus and told him and his wife they could have a seat in the back. Yogi said, "No, no, no, I will sit in the front with you." I had one of the most amazing, blown-away conversations with him for about 20 minutes. It was great because he was someone I grew up watching with my family.

Can you describe a memorable moment?

So, one day we were having an event in a dry state. I remember one of the stars there was John O'Hurley (*Seinfeld*), a man invited to every golf tournament; he was the life of the party, a good friend, an incredible husband, actor, singer, and golfer. We had just finished the golf tournament and were entering into the evening festivities of dinner and music. The bar was shutting down and yet no one wanted to stop drinking, they just wanted to keep on partying. Something that David always told me was to take care of the talent, give them what they want, and to not take no for an answer when trying to do that.

I walked myself up to the bar and told the bartender, "Hey listen, all these people still want to drink, they are having a great time and can't you just stay open?" Bartender said, "No, it's a dry state, it's the law." I just didn't know what to do! I went up to David and told him what was happening. He was completely unaffected by this situation and said, "Go get my briefcase." I open up the brief case and there was about 50 mini liquor bottles. I proceeded to give them out throughout the night, continuing the party until dawn.

David was always very calculated. He anticipated everything. It was a great educational foundation for me. I learned more with David than with any education my parents paid for through college. David is a forward thinker, as is Richard Branson, who I now work for at *VIRGIN*.

How long did you work for David?
It was till about 98-99. Even after I stopped working for David, David still proceeded to still ask me to attend about 10 events a year, which I did. My schedule became overwhelming with other things that were happening in my life, and, while I loved running around with celebrities and carrying golf bags, I wasn't able to moonlight anymore.

What did you learn most from David Mirisch?
One of my learning foundations is that nothing is impossible, dreaming is believing. I learned that if you are persistent and you believe something is going to happen, then it is possible. It was a lot of work being David's assistant and that might be why I am so hard on my assistants; never except the word no. Turn that "No" into a "Yes." Somehow, someway, there is always a way. David is in the problem-solving business; nothing is impossible, just know the problems, identify them, and then

everything else will work itself out. Assure the team is working hard but having fun, while at the same time growing the brand. David always wanted a quality product; that was every event he did. With a happy team the end product will be fantastic. You know, David never worried about how much money he was going to make doing the events he did, it was always how much the charity was going to make. I watched David so many times take no money for his events. That says a lot right there.

Hal Linden Interview (Barney Miller)

Hal is a man that would go to David's charity events…a lot of times it was golf tournaments that he was a part of. Many times he would "sing for his super." After the tournaments, David would have a dinner and a spontaneous show of some sort, with people such as Hal and Pat Boone just getting up and playing or singing something. Nothing was ever really planned in that way, however everything always ran smoothly and everything that was scheduled was always on time, just the way it should be. Other people that sang at the golf tournaments were Peter Marshall and Jerry Vale, Pat Boone, Alan Thicke.

Sometimes having dinner with the contributors gave way into putting on a show, sometimes it would be rehearsed, and sometimes it would be off-the-cuff. Hal played the clarinet and sang. There was one time where David had a trio and Hal just got up on stage and started playing his clarinet in the background. He had also played with Les Brown and Ray McKinley bands during his career.

Hal traveled with David to Malaysia and played in a charity golf tournament for the king and queen of Malaysia. On the first par there was a sign that said beware of rocks and cobras. The queen seemed like she hadn't played that much golf, she had someone tee up for her and when she hit the ball, the drive wasn't very long. It mainly just skimmed the ground and then the crowd would just applaud. On that same day, Hal hit the ball and when it landed a monkey picked it up and ran off with it.

Cynthia Interview, Former wife and Mother of Michael

Cynthia was raised Mormon, grew up poor and was one of seven kids from Brea. She was in beauty pageants, was Miss Photogenic. The photographer who was taking her pictures knew David. She wanted to get into commercials and he got her in contact with David. Cynthia went into David's office on a Saturday; his office was on Sunset Blvd. She was dressed prim and proper in her own eyes, because that's how she was raised. He seemed nice, a funny kind of guy. When she sat down and was sitting in front of his desk he threw down a magazine. On the cover was Raquel Welch (*1 Million Years BC*) and he looked at her and said "You can either go in this direction or in the penthouse direction."

A few days later (it was a Tuesday) she got a call from David asking her out for dinner with his family. It was a dinner party with some of the top production people in the city, on Coldwater Canyon. Cynthia was star-struck and was just in awe over it all. Later that week he invited her to his house to swim with the family as well. Being raised Mormon she had no Jewish people around her, and she had no connection to the people she was surrounding herself with besides the fact that David liked her.

Cynthia and David met in July and they married on Oct 2nd 1965, and though she was in love with him, she was also in love with the "it" of it all and the life to be had with him. They were married for eight years. She looks at him with love still in her eyes, but just in a different way, like brother and sister. The trust is there still after all these years. He's the same person from 50 years ago, he's very stable, what you see is what you get, no evil bone in his body. He might at times be narcissistic, but he's still a good man.

With Good Friend Steve Garvey

With Charleton Heston — Stars Hall of Fame Orlando, Florida

United Artists, Mirisch moved on to industry giant, Rogers and Cowan. David recalls, "I got my training under Henry Rogers, where I spent a year in his office just sitting in a corner, at a little desk. I had to come in every morning by 7 A.M., and I had to have every newspaper and magazine read, with every Rogers and Cowan client underlined. And that's why I still come in at 5 and 6 every morning — I got into a rut!" After leaving Rogers and Cowan, David began his own public relations firm. Today, after several partners throughout the years, he is running the firm alone . . . on an international level.

Mirisch discovered Farrah Fawcett by judging a Texas Beauty Pageant she was in. He has represented and helped build the careers of Omar Shariff, the late Peter Sellers, Racquel Welch, Merv Griffin, Athletes Ken Stabler, Wilt Chamberlin, Tony Trabert and music's Kenny Rogers, Pat Boone, The Fifth Dimension, and many more. In addition, he has represented countless production companies and numerous corporate accounts. "Everyone needs a P.R. man, you can't exist without one," explains Mirisch.

Charity organizations agree . . . in the past ten years, David has organized, planned and created over 150 celebrity charity events, raising over 4 million dollars. His favorite events are celebrity tennis, golf and skiing tournaments. "Celebrities love to compete," says Mirisch, "I guess it's in their blood, but they also like to lend themselves to solid charitable events. For the most part, celebrities feel an obligation to give something back to what the public has given them, and a charitable sporting event fills that void exactly. Their competitive spirit is quenched, and they can get away from the hassles of Hollywood. David's greatest satisfaction comes from "being able to see a charity raise much more money than they ever expected."

Because of his talented knack for organizing major celebrity-charity sporting events, and publicizing the many famous faces that lend themselves to A Day In The Sun, David's phone never stops ringing . . . from charity organizations, to corporations, to the fans, and including the celebrities, such as Pat Boone who attends "To benefit charity, and see friends in the business who he hasn't seen due to conflicting schedules . . . David makes a great Mother Hen."

David's stature in the entertainment industry places him in a position of preeminence in the entertainment field. Newcomers to the industry constantly seek advice from this wise and sage man only having to look at his long and illustrious career in the public relations sphere. Mirisch reflects, "On choosing the right public relations firm for yourself, you must consider your budget, and what your needs are. It's appropriate to ask for a client list if it's a new P.R. firm, and if the names are not recognizable, to call one of the clients and see what the company

has done for them." Once signed with an agency, "It's important to remember that a new client needs about two to three months of organizational time. Organizational time is defined as the time it takes to develop the 'personality' — to get the right photos, and do mailings. This is all part of making people aware that the client exists," says Mirisch.

P.R. firms are a vehicle for the newcomer and or seasoned veteran to keep in the public limelight. The responsibility of the P.R. firm varies from client to client; and, accordingly the rates charged differ from role to role. For example, a lead in a T.V. series might pay $1,500.00 per month, where a newcomer might pay about $500.00 . . . some P.R. agencies work on percentage, but as Mirisch states, "Remember you get what you pay for . . . public relations can only open the door for you." Mirisch continued, "If you're completely new to the industry, and you don't know a soul, take your time. Get into workshops, classes, small theater groups — find a friend that knows the industry and can guide you properly, makingsure you don't make the wrong moves . . . read the trades, go on interviews, get composites, a good resume, go out on calls . . . get out there! If you have credits and no money for a publicist, convince someone to work for you for a percentage . . . most importantly, if you don't have anything good to say, don't say it . . . it is a very small industry."

Being at the right place, at the right time is definitely a start, then, it's all up to you, you either make it, or you don't. In the case of David Mirisch, he's made it to the top . . . a wonderful wife and family, an every-growing business, celebrity friends, the respect of the entertainment industry, and a creative mind that just won't quit!

David Mirisch article

Ironically enough, nothing happened to her career-wise. It was only the love they shared for each other and the marriage they had. He spoiled her rotten and she lived in this great fantasy that it wasn't until it was all over and she met reality.

Alan Campbell: Jake and the Fatman

He was a theatre actor but got into sitcoms in 1984: *Three's a Crowd,* a spin off from the hit series *Three's Company,* it was the only TV series he ever did; It was also the first of any kind of LA media he was involved in, and after the series started David invited him to golf and tennis events. He was rated as one of the better tennis players on the Mirisch celebrity circuit.

A Talk With Baseball Legend, Steve Garvey

David Mirisch has been a master of celebrity events since the 60's, creating associations between stars and charities — from tennis, golf, bowling, to basketball. Actors, singers, and athletes always love working with David. He would give celebrities a chance to work together in an entertaining format. Nobody said no to David Mirisch. David has a gift of creating a pleasurable experiences for everyone involved and he does everything with grace, charm, and persistence. In an exclusive interview for our book, Los Angeles Dodgers All-Star, Steve Garvey, offered insights on working with David.

Tell me about your very first experience meeting David Mirisch, the first thing you did with him and all those things.
Steve: Looking back, it was a charity event where we first met, back in the 70's. Subsequently, David, who said that there was a concept of

an off-season travelling basketball team playing for charity, and would I be interested in this. Yeah, I played in high school and college a little bit, intramurals. Thought it would be a great way for us to stay in shape and raise money for the high schools in Southern California, and that's when we started to see each other on a kind of regular basis. And, the evolution was the team had not only some Dodger greats on it, but some great entertainers in that era who have gone on to be significant – television, movies, and sports stars.

Basically, after you'd finished playing with the Dodgers, right?
Steve: I was still playing for the Dodgers when I'd first started.

You were kind of doing both?
Steve: Yeah. Exactly.

That's great. So you had the time to do this, go back to training and kind of do a back and forth.
Steve: Yeah it was in the off-season. We played 21 games each year at high schools in and around Southern California They would be the recipients for the funds raised for the evening, and we would play against the coaches and alumni of that school, and we were made up of athletes and entertainers.

Can you name me some of the people that you were playing with?
Steve: Oh, gosh, Mark Harmon (*CSI:*), I remember clearly was one of the point guards with me. There was also Denzel Washington, Richard Dean Anderson (*McGyver*). Then we had J.J. from *Good Times*, Jimmy Walker, Actor Ron Masak, Jack Coleman (*Dynasty*), and many more,

including singer Pat Boone. But the most important thing was David. He was the organizer. He did a great job, got the best sponsors, and we ate at the best restaurants before the game. We would travel as far as Oxnard, Camarillo, San Fernando Valley, and Orange County, and it was a lot of fun. One time we went to China Lake Navy Base, three hours away.

Who was the coach of the team?
Steve: Well, it was — you know, David was kind of the GM, kind of worked the sidelines. We all kind of jumped in. Somebody was out of breath and somebody would take their place, but ironically David Mirisch was a caretaker. Trying to keep everybody from running out of breath, pulling a muscle. David did an amazing job. Working the sidelines, he had a little help. But essentially, he was. David had a great understanding relationship with the team. Not only the team, but with the entertainment community, and also the sport community.

Was there a captain?
Steve: I was basically the captain of the team. I want to say Mark Harmon, more on the celebrity side, was a very good athlete, as he played for UCLA. Glenn Burke was another guy with the Dodgers that played with us. David was the brainchild of all this. We only lost twice. We lost once to a San Fernando high school team. They brought in three guys from USC. They played basketball four to five years. It was a rough night for us.

Oh, well, losing once is not bad, you know? Our record that year was 19 to 2

Well, you know what happened? We'd start off against the high school coaches, they were brought in to practice and we go two and twelve, fifteen to one, and begin to gradually slowly get into it, you know, challenge our competitive nature, and we'd end up winning and pulling away at the end.

David was on the sidelines, you know, most of those games where we'd jump off to a ten or fifteen-point deficit he would give us a little pep talk. He would try to challenge us, well I guess our competitive nature. You know, he was so good at it. And of course, spent his life organizing charity events and got people in the community involved with everything he did.

We played for about 7 years. But I have to say, working with David was always an amazing experience.

David Mirisch, Linda Evans

Petula Clark, David Mirisch, Kathryn Grayson

Johnny Mathis, David Mirisch

The Fifth Dimension, David Mirisch

David Mirisch, Charleton Heston

Jonathan Winters, David Mirisch

David and Sandy in Denmark with Dionne Warwick

Sonny and Cher, David Mirisch

David Mirisch, John Forsythe

Drummer Buddy Rich, David Mirisch

Barbara Stanwyck, David Mirisch

Buddy Hackett,
David Mirisch

The Mills Brothers, David Mirisch

Duke Ellington,
David Mirisch

Dionne Warwick,
David Mirisch

Ann-Margret,
David Mirisch

Zsa Zsa Gabor,
David Mirisch

Jerry Lewis,
David Mirisch

David Mirisch, Milton Berle

David and Sandy with *Golden Girls'* Estelle Getty

"The Duke of PR" David Mirisch with "The Duke" John Wayne

Vanna White, David Mirisch

David Mirisch, Gregory Peck

Chill Wills, David Mirisch

Trini Lopez,
David Mirisch

David Mirisch, Shaquille O'Neal

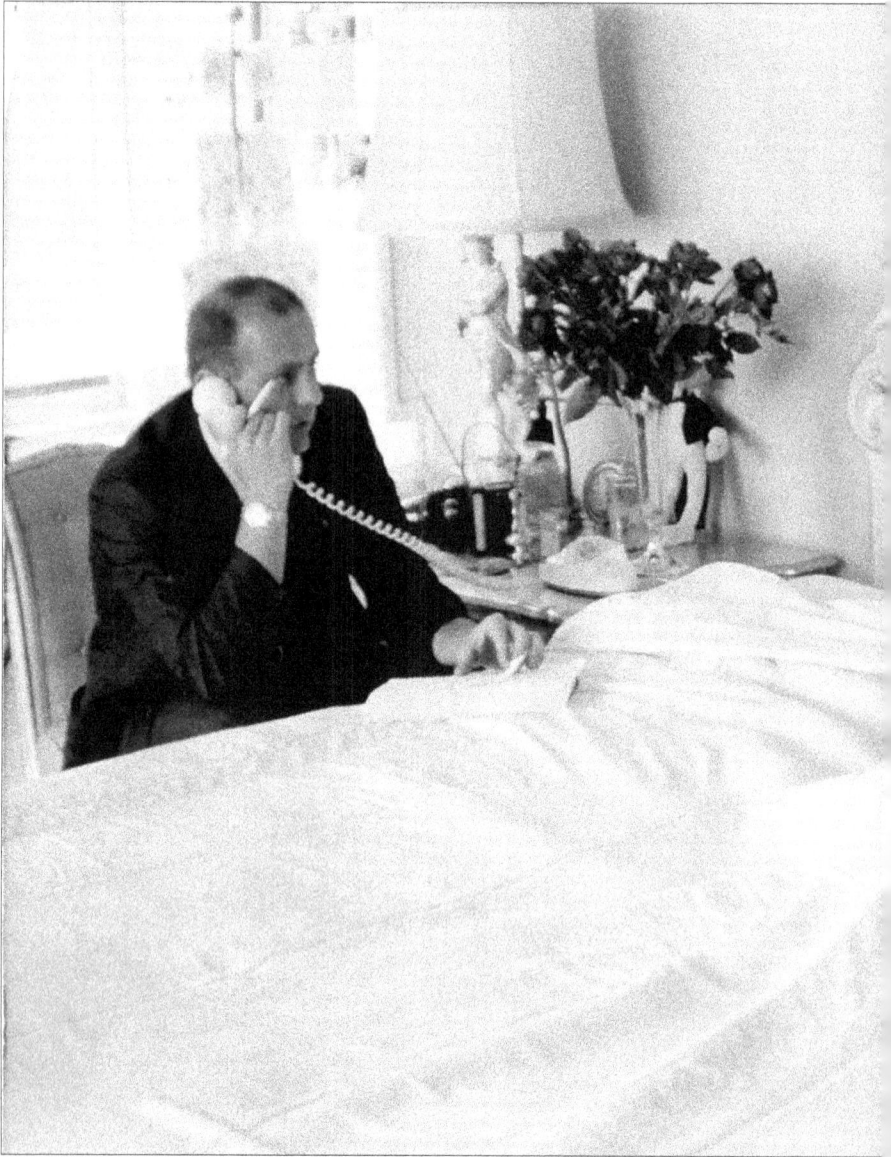

Peter Sellers, Britt Ekland

David Mirisch, James Caan

Marty Allen, Mike Connors, David Mirisch, Buddy Hackett, Jonathan Winters

Eddie Fischer,
David Mirisch

Joe Louis, David Mirisch

David Mirisch, Herb Alpert

David Mirisch and The Hollywood Deb Stars

David Mirisch, Jesse Owens

David Mirisch and The Harlem Globetrotters

Bobby Mirisch, David Mirisch and Gary Cooper

Donna Douglas
from *The Beverly
Hillbillies*

Leonard Nimoy
and David
Mirisch

David Mirisch,
Robert Mitchum

Gene Autry and
David Mirisch

Jim Nabors and David Mirisch

Grammy Winner
Debby Boone,
David Mirisch

Lawrence Welk,
David Mirisch

Peter Sellers leaving the hospital with wife Britt Ekland and David Mirisch

Willie Mays,
David Mirisch

David Mirisch, John McEnroe

Stella Stevens, David Mirisch

David and Sandy with Olympic Skier, Bill Johnson

David Mirisch,
Muhammad Ali

Margaux Hemingway,
David Mirisch

Julie Andrews with David and Sandy

Britt Ekland, David Mirisch

David Mirisch with Ted Williams .406 bat

Hank Aaron,
David Mirisch

David Mirisch,
Roy Clark

Barbi Benton,
David Mirisch

Above: David Mirisch with California Governor Pat Brown

Cornel Wilde, David Mirisch

Ironsides'
Barbara Anderson,
David Mirisch

Frank Lovejoy, David Mirisch

Don Ho,
David Mirisch

Tony Trabert Tournament, David's First Tennis Tournament

David Mirisch,
Jack Lemmon

Celebrity sports producer David Mirisch (kneeling, second from the left), with a group of world class athletes who participated in one of his recent celebrity tennis tournaments. Bottom Row (L-R): Football player Otis McKinney, Olympic pole vaulter Bob Seagren and Water polo player David Burke. Top Row: Football player Johnnie Johnson, Olympic skier Bill Johnson, Olympic diver Dr. Sammy Lee, Hockey player Marcel Dionne, Olympic synchronized swimmer Cany Costie-Burke and Football player Dennis Thurman. In the Back Row: Basketball player Reggie Theus.

David Mirisch – Celebrity Athlete Tennis Tournament

Howard Cossell,
David Mirisch

Karen Valentine,
David Mirisch

David Mirisch,
Arthur Ashe

Yogi Berra,
David Mirisch

Olympic Swimming
Champion Mark
Spitz, David Mirisch

Bobby Orr,
David Mirisch

"Dr. J",
Julius Erving and
David Mirisch

David Mirisch, Bobby Riggs

Sugar Ray Robinson, David Mirisch

Sugar Ray
Leonard,
David Mirisch

David Mirisch
at camp

David Mirisch as child

David Mirisch,
Joe Frazier

Evander Holyfield, David Mirisch

Willie Shoemaker,
David Mirisch

David Mirisch,
McKenzie
Westmore

Celebrity Golf

Film and television celebrities arrived from the United States on April 26 for the Garuda Indonesia Celebrity Golf Tournament held at the Tanah Merah Country Club and the Charity Gala Dinner at the Hyatt Regency. Funds exceeding $116,000 were raised during the gala dinner for the Home Nursing Foundation, the National Heart Association, the National Kidney Foundation and the Seah Cheng Siang Memorial Fund.

Ms Lucie Wilson, Mr Rafiq Jumabhoy, Ms Margaux Hemingway and Mr Robert Dawson

Mr Keith Chua, Mr Ernesto A'de Lima and Ms Joyce Dewitt

Ms Khrystyne Haje and Mr David Mirisch

Mr David Soul and Ms Regina Lesslar

Mr Arthur Holliger

Ms Karen Robert, Mr Douglas Benjamin, Ms Irene Lim and Ms Mona Melwani

Ms Lee Siok Tin and Ms Karen Dawson

David Mirisch Golf Article

109

YOU CAN BECOME A "SOMEBODY" LIKE FARRAH
The man who discovered her tells how

DAVID MIRISCH

Farrah Fawcett,
David Mirisch

Exclusive pix from Mirisch's files show Farrah at start of Hollywood career.

What did this girl have that marked her for future superstardom?

Farrah Fawcett

David Mirisch in his only movie, *Beachhead* (1955)

David and Ripon College Cheerleaders

A TRIBUTE TO

Walter Mirisch

A Producer For All Seasons

"Picture making is largely a function of relationships. The idea that talented people can come together, complement one another's efforts and resolve that they want to work together is fundamental to motion picture making."
—Walter Mirisch

WISCONSIN
FiLM
FESTIVAL

March 30-April 2, 2000

David Mirisch, Barry Williams and Bruce Jenner

David Mirisch, Barbara Eden and Merv Griffin

Jimmy Connors,
David Mirisch

Beauty at a Hollywood Ball

UPI Telephoto

Blonde actress Debbie Reynolds, president of the Thalians, a Hollywood charity organization, greets actor Omar Sharif and actress Anjanette Comer at the 13th annual Thalians' Ball in Beverly Hills. Composed of some 200 members, mostly from the entertainment industry, the organization currently is building a health center for the mentally ill.

Debbie Reynolds and Anjanette Comer

David Mirisch,
a proud graduate

David Mirisch graduation

David's home and David shooting a commercial

David at his home doing a television interview

David Mirisch and *Young and the Restless* veteran Kate Linder

Chapter 1:

Encounters with the King and The Chairman of the Board

GROUNDBREAKING ARTIST AND Grammy Lifetime Achievement Award winning Elvis Presley was certainly known as the "King of Rock and Roll." David Mirisch could also be called the king in his own way. He was the master of event planning and promotion; and he did it better than anyone else.

David would encounter Elvis Presley in the late 60's in Las Vegas. David's and Elvis' paths unexpectedly crossed when David's friend, Frank Lieberman, a writer for the *Los Angeles Herald Examiner*, came to Las Vegas to interview Elvis. David and his wife Cynthia were invited to join Frank at a show. Following Elvis' concert, Frank invited them to join him at Elvis' suite in the Las Vegas Hilton.

This immaculate suite had 7 bedrooms, 8 bathrooms, and 3 bars. The view from the balcony was breathtaking.

When David and Cynthia arrived, Frank introduced them to Elvis and Priscilla. What seemed like catching up with old friends; the six of them talked for hours about movies, the industry, and particularly martial arts, which Elvis was a huge and practicing enthusiast fan. The Mirisch family had produced two movies that Elvis starred in called

Kid Galahad and *Follow That Dream*. An immediate rapport between David and Elvis was quickly developed.

Meanwhile, Cynthia and Priscilla found instant chemistry towards one another. The experience of being young brides to iconic men in show business left both women sharing the same trepidation and anxieties. Swapping newlywed stories, Cynthia shared with Priscilla her anxiety of being a new bride and being thrown into David's extremely busy career. Priscilla was feeling the same; after all, she was married to Elvis (The King of Rock and Roll), one the most successful and beloved icons of all time. Let's not forget his reputation with women.

One of the most difficult things for the two brides was they needed to be "ON" all the time, constantly meeting new people, including the press, packing and unpacking suitcases, and being so far away from normalcy. They weren't your typical 60's housewives.

As the night grew long, drinks were married with shared conversations until six in the morning. David and his wife, Cynthia, would never see Elvis or Priscilla Presley again. This night, unlike any other was extraordinarily unforgettable for the two of them.

Meeting The Chairman of the Board

Iconic Frank Sinatra is probably the most famous pop, jazz vocalist of all time. He is an Academy Award and Grammy Lifetime Achievement Award winner and is celebrated all over the world.

While David Mirisch was organizing one of his events for the Tina Sinatra Youth Center Celebrity Tennis Tournament at the Palm Desert Racquet Club in Palm Springs, several celebrities in television and film were scheduled to appear.

It was rumored that Frank Sinatra was going to make a surprise appearance. Surprisingly, at the last minute, Frank joined the event.

Frank Sinatra and David

Frank Sinatra and David

David personally took care of Frank Sinatra, at his request. For David, even though he had worked with so many legends in his career, this was a great honor. Frank talked to David about his music, his films, his friends, like: Dean Martin, Sammy Davis Jr., Peter Lawford; they also talked about some of his favorite film costars from Doris Day to Debbie Reynolds. Spending the day with Mr. Sinatra was intriguingly interesting.

Sinatra had an impressive entourage of people around him, including his bodyguard and personal staff. David was certainly challenged taking care of such an overwhelming group. For him it was a rewarding experience, but by the end of the day, and like his night with Elvis, this is something that will be carved forever in David Mirisch history.

Pat Boone, a legendary music career with a glass of milk.
David Mirisch had so many relationships with legendary celebrities. Several celebrities have been with him since day one and have participated in all his events: from Connie Stevens, Donna Mills, Alan Thicke, and several more. Music legend Pat Boone formed an incredible friendship with David. Pat was always willing to participate with any charity David was putting together. At some point, Pat revealed during an interview for this book that David had booked him on three separate events at the same time; luckily, they were all in the same city. Pat Boone is known in the world of music for hits on the charts including "Two Hearts," "Aint That A Shame," and "I'll Be Home."

Pat Boone has conquered the world of pop through the 50s, 60s, and 70s, and he even crossed over into heavy metal. Pat's life was always conducted with a strong religious faith that helped his life and career through some difficult times, including his grandson's accident. When this happened, David was the first to come and decided to help

Pat in an annual golf tournament that would benefit traumatic brain injury victims. More celebrities were happy to come together to play golf for this tournament. Pat Boone had been so generous to so many of them for many years.

Pat Boone, David Mirisch

Pat Boone, David Mirisch

The tournament became an annual success and is still running until this day. David even produced Pat's first tournament for Bethel Bible School in Chattanooga, Tennessee, where they brought down 25 stars and had a police escort from the plane to their hotel right down Main Street. Pat showed his deep friendship to David when he did the eulogy at Sandy's mother's (Toni Kelman) service. They are both the same age and still see each other on a fairly regular basis.

From Sweetness to Greatness

E.J. Peaker was the Broadway star from the show *Hello! Dolly*, as well as the film adaptation. She also starred in her own Emmy nominated series *That's Life* with Robert Morse. The entrance to her diversified career was meeting David Mirisch. When E.J. described meeting David for this book, it was a very moving experience for her. Coming from Tulsa, Oklahoma and being chosen by David for the Hollywood DEB Star Ball for young performers was the chance for a lifetime. She would eventually have an important career as a frequent guest on several television series including *That Girl*, *Route 66*, *The Odd Couple*, *Love: American Style*, and more than 20 appearances with Johnny Carson on *The Tonight Show*. She said David made her who she is today.

Chapter 2:

David Touring Communist China

DAVID QUICKLY WENT through his golden Rolodex of celebrities. It took him 6 months of phone call requests to acquire some very special celebrities. The celebrities that starred in *Cycling Through China* were:

Lorne Green – David had been friends with Lorne for many years. Lorne was internationally known as the star of the TV series *Bonanza* and then *Battlestar Galactica*. He had hosted a few celebrity events for David. David will always remember one specific memorable event, the event in Colorado Springs where they took a tour of NORAD and had lunch with 5,000 Air Force cadets from the United States Air Force Academy. He was one of the nicest men David had met in his 50 years of show business. So, when this project needed a "headliner" David immediately thought of him. Lorne and his wife, Nancy, joined David and the rest of the cast and crew halfway through the trip. He narrated footage as they visited community by community, and each wonderful tourist attraction they visited as well. When the group arrived in Canton, Lorne was the co-host of the final show in front of 5,000 people. David loved Lorne dearly as a friend.

Ben Vereen – David knew he needed a variety headliner like Ben Vereen. Ben was a highly-respected Tony Award winner on Broadway

for his starring role in *Pippin*. He was also in the highly-acclaimed production of *Roots*. During the cast and crew time in China, Ben was
always the lead cyclist. He was probably in the best physical condition
of any of them. Besides entertaining the group in friendly sessions, he
was a wonderful addition to the special. David gave him a video camera. He took videos of the people and they could not believe that they
could see themselves.

Lindsay Bloom David wanted to bring a beauty queen and a county
western performer. So, he chose the just married couple of Lindsay
Bloom and Mayf Nutter. Lindsay was a former Miss Utah and Miss
USA. She had a successful acting career appearing on *The Dean
Martin Show, Six Pack Annie, Cover Girl Models, Hughes and Harlow,*
and *Angels in Hell* (playing the role of Jean Healow). Then, she landed
the role of Mike Hammer's secretary in the TV series *Mickey Spillane's
Mike Hammer*.

Mayf Nutter – Mayf was the youngest honoree in the Nashville
Country Hall of Fame's Walkway of Stars. He and Lindsay (his wife)
have lived in Bakersfield, California for many years where he performed at Buck Owens Crystal Palace. He has performed with Merle
Haggard, Kenny Rogers, Del Shannon, and many other country music
greats. Plus, he has recorded his own albums. While in China, he and
Lindsay performed their songs to the delight of thousands of Chinese
people that had never heard of their kind of music. They were the perfect married couple to bring along.

Paul Horn – Paul has been recognized as one of the greatest flutists
of all time. He had worked with Nat King Cole, Duke Ellington, Cal

Tjader, Chico Hamilton, and Tony Bennett. Producer David Wolper produced a documentary on Paul called *Portrait of A Jazz Musician*. His playing his flute all over China was a wonderful experience for the people of China.

Brandon Scott and Mark Wenzel David felt to round out his entertainment presentation he needed to bring two types of entertainment that were familiar to the people of China; magic and mimes. So, he reached out to two of his acquaintances (that are still friends today) magician Brandon Scott and the mime, Mark Wenzel. They both did an amazing job of entertaining people as the group visited each commune during their three-week bicycle ride from Macau to Canton, where they put on the final show. David has wonderful memories of children laughing without Mark uttering a sound. He clearly remembers Brandon levitating Lindsay Bloom up from two chairs without using his hands or arms; the Chinese had never seen this kind of act before.

David Hume Kennerly – David was an award-winning photographer and shot for *TIME Magazine*. The producers of the show brought him into the project. The crew and cast were very lucky to have him as part of the team. Besides taking great photographs of their trip, he literally saved David Mirisch's recollections of the trip. David had purchased a new camera for the trip and was taking some nice pictures in the first few days. Then something happened...He was riding his bike over a cobblestone street and all of a sudden, his camera popped out of his basket, fell to the ground and broke. There they were, hundreds of miles from a city and no one to fix his camera. David K. happened to have an extra camera and loaned it to David. Thus, allowing David

Mirisch to take the hundreds of pictures that he still has in his collection today.

Joe Cunningham – Joe played basketball with the Harlem Globetrotters in the 1960's. He was 6'7" and had attended Winston Salem University. David personally reached out to the Globetrotters office and asked who would be a great "Ambassador of America," and to basketball. They said Joe Cunningham. Most people in China, at that time, had never seen a black man, never the less one who stood to be 6'7". Joe was an immediate hit with all of the people of China. David gave him a Polaroid camera and he continually took pictures of the people and printed those pictures to give to the Chinese people to keep. It can be assumed that those people and their families still have those pictures to this day.

Kate Jackson An American actress, director, and producer famously known for *Charlies Angels*. She is a three time Emmy Award nominee and four time Golden Globe Award nominee. Kate was assigned as the narrator for the special and made short appearances in the documentary. Kate had to be carefully edited in postproduction because she could only spend two days in China. The rest of the cast became very committed in the project and cycled to predestinated cities that were assigned for the trip.

From a viewer's perspective, it was interesting to get a glimpse of this unknown world. The focus was put on the children of China laughing and enjoying the experience of curious Americans visiting them.

Chapter 3:

David Mirisch: Creating Press Path for Pink Panther

Before Mary Harts' *Entertainment Tonight, E Entertainment, Access Hollywood*, entertainment was meagerly covered. Fans would get their news from monthly publications, like *Photoplay* or *Rona Barrett's Hollywood*. Most celebrities in the 40's, 50's, 60's, and 70's had publicists that took care of all the information going out to the press. Publicists knew their clients so well that they often facilitated most interviews for the stars they represented.

Golden Globe winner Peter Sellers is probably one of the most beloved entertainment actors ever to come out of England and crash Hollywood. His memorable character, "Inspector Clouseau," role in the *Pink Panther* movies made his work legendary. Peter was often credited as the greatest comedian of all time and was an incredible actor with great depth. In 1964 the Mirisch Corp. had asked Peter to take part in their Dean Martin, Kim Novak film *Kiss Me Stupid*. He arrived stateside, excited to be in this film. Unfortunately, Peter suffered a massive heart attack when he landed in Los Angeles. He was quickly taken to Cedars Sinai Medical Center for major surgery. David Mirisch was immediately assigned to take care of Peter and inform the press of Peter's affairs and progress. This was a disturbing major event for a well beloved emerging Hollywood Star. David handled this assignment with diplomacy and discretion; which was not easy. David had to balance the demands of the public relations of Peter and his wife, Britt Ekland.

Peter Sellers and David Mirisch

Peter often described himself as a "hopeless romantic" who was constantly falling in love. In 1964, shortly after the triumphs as "Inspector Clouseau," he married Swedish actress Britt Ekland after an 11 day courtship. Shortly afterward, he suffered his first major heart attack.

Stories were emerging from every direction in the press. Rumors good and bad were spreading out rapidly, and Peter Sellers had a reputation of not being in the best of terms with the press. David handled the challenge of slaying and putting all of the rumors to rest with "*a plomb."* When Peter started recovering he was confined to bed rest, with his wife at his side. Keeping the heart attack a secret, David would conduct all the interviews and arranged all of Peter's PR needs at his bedside.

Keeping his surgery under wraps became a little more complicated when Peter became unavailable for a longer period of time; since he was still expected to star in *Kiss Me Stupid.* Unfortunately, his role had to be replaced by Emmy Award winning Ray Walston, who was best known for *My Favorite Martian; Caprice* with Doris Day and Richard Harris; *Fast Times at Ridgemont High* with Sean Penn. A story started circulating that Peter was very unhappy with the treatment he was receiving in Hollywood, in particularly from Cedars-Sinai Medical Center, which was completely untrue. David had to quickly turn the rumor around and emphasized that Peter was getting ready to do another outing with Inspector Clouseau in *A Shot in the Dark.* Meanwhile, a true friendship was built between David, Peter, and Britt.

Peter left LA fully recovered and happy with Los Angeles, thanks to David. Below is the press release and letters that were exchanged between David, Peter, and the press during this hectic time.

Los Angeles Rams Cheerleaders -1978

Of the many promotions and productions that David was involved in. His biggest was in 1978 when he created the very first cheerleading squad of the Los Angeles Rams. The story in itself is quite interesting. He had been a cheerleader at Ripon College, and for 28 years produced the California State High School Cheerleading Championships at Six Flags Magic Mountain, so he knew quite a bit about the world of cheerleading. One day he got an appointment with Mr. Carroll Rosenbloom, the owner of the Rams. He went into his office and said "Mr. Rosenbloom, we have the most beautiful women in the world here in Los Angeles. Why are the Dallas Cowboys the only team in the National Football League that has a professional cheerleading team?" They talked for a few minutes and Mr. Rosenbloom said, "Okay, go put one together."

So, David, through the publicity department of the Rams, got the announcement of the tryouts in to every paper in Southern California. On the first weekend in March, 850 young women showed up at the Los Angeles Coliseum to be members of that first squad. David put together a distinguished panel of 25 judges that included friends like Wilt Chamberlain, Jim Hill, Ed Arnold, Dwight Stones, Lindsay Bloom, Dough Krikorian, and Bruce Wayne of *KFI In the Sky*. That day they ended up with 50 finalists that were eventually cut down to the final 28. Two of the gals that went on to entertainment fame were Jenilee Harrison of *Three's Company* and Patty Kotero of *Apollonia 6* and *Purple Rain*, who jawere in the press and media every day. They were "the talk of Los Angeles."

On the day the team was formally introduced, David was able to get Mayor Tom Bradley to come out and welcome the girls to their new positions. Unfortunately, David was only with them for two exhibition games. He was called into a Ram executive office and was told, "Thanks for a great job in assembling the team, but we're going to take it over from here." Since David, being the good and honest guy that he is, he assumed a handshake with Mr. Rosenbloom was binding, but it wasn't. David had nothing in writing so he had no recourse. He told me he learned from that lesson. But, in the spring of 2016, he assembled 21 of the original 28 gals to a big Sunday afternoon reunion at the Boathouse in Long Beach. Most of the gals had not seen each other in THIRTY-EIGHT YEARS!. Everyone laughed and cried that afternoon, and, David was "toasted" numerous times that day by gals that are now friends for the rest of their lives. A job well done, David.

Chapter 4:

Hollywood vs. Wives

MANAGING A CAREER in Hollywood is a difficult task, especially when raising a family. David Mirisch was lucky enough to be married to 3 wonderful women, who, in their own way, made his life more pleasurable and easier to live. David was first married to Tina Walsh in 1959, while beginning his journey and adventure through Hollywood. Tina gave David a wonderful daughter by the name of Angela. She was instrumental in guiding Angela through some difficult growing years while David was travelling. Their separation was hard on the marriage. David felt in 1965 that it was time to move on.

He then married Cynthia Ann Green on October 2nd, 1965. The young, beautiful bride was literally thrown into David's world. Dealing with celebrity events, parties at David's home, children that were growing up, and dealing with her own personal crises. At some point, Cynthia found solace in meeting Priscilla Presley, mentioned earlier in the book. Cynthia was hoping that a friendship with Priscilla would develop after that meeting, however it never materialized. Her life was literally overwhelmed with activities; something that she was not prepared for. In retrospect, she felt that she was part of a great experience, but might have been too young to truly appreciate it.

In the 70's David met Sandra Kelman. She was known as the

youngest franchised film and television agent in Hollywood, specializing in superstar kids like Lance Kerwin. She built the careers of such child actors as Academy Award Winners Jodie Foster and Barry Williams, Chris Knight, Maureen McCormack and Susan Olsen of the *Brady Bunch*, Larry Wilcox of *Chips*, Willie Aames of *Eight is Enough*, and many others.

Sandy was part of Hollywood's DNA. Hollywood was her backyard. She knew how to make the system work for herself, her agency, and her clients. She had carte blanche to walk into any studio and every producer's office in Hollywood to present a client. Not aggressively, but with charm, grace, and style. She developed a mutual respect between the actors and the studios. Her actors worked constantly. At one point, she had 26 kids under series contract. Early on, when she couldn't get hold of a feature film script, David Mirisch was the one she called. He always pulled through for Sandy.

A friendship developed between David and Sandy that slowly grew into love. This was the first time that David developed a relationship with someone equally important in Hollywood as he was, but in a different field. With perfect chemistry between the two, they challenged each other to achieve even more. It took some time for the two to get married. For David and Sandy, the third time was a charm! Sandy had a 3-year-old daughter, Summer, by a previous marriage and, on August 18th, 1991, David and Sandy took their vows at Flathead Lake, Montana. Sandy stepped away from casting but stayed very involved in the industry and started helping David with all of the charity events he was working on. The two of them formed a very solid union. A delightful job of putting difficult projects together. With the amount of celebrities that David had acquired through the last 50 years and the relationships Sandy had built with her clients in Hollywood, they

PR to the Stars

received free reign on connecting celebrities to different projects; they had free reign connecting celebrities to numerous projects. Doing so with charm and grace, it became impossible to say no to them.

Chapter 5:

Kids vs. Fame

RAISING CHILDREN IS a difficult task no matter where you are in the world. In Hollywood, the challenges are a bit different and David's three children Angela, Michael, and Summer had to deal with many unforeseen obstacles. David's career often came at the forefront of everything he did. Having three wives and the addition of children seemed like a casual thing in Hollywood, but it wasn't for him. Angela, Michael, and Summer dealt with unusual issues growing up. Their father, who was promoting celebrities, hosting events, and traveling all over the world made things a bit difficult for them. The children never lacked of anything; they all attended the best schools, had a lot of interesting friends, and of course the regular ups and downs of growing up. Everything became available to them, including dealing with substance abuse.

Screaming for independence during their teen years and the ins and outs of relationships of their own as they were growing up; no matter what, they always relied on David to get them out of any situation they put themselves in, and he never failed them and he was always there. This included phone calls in the middle of the night, picking up Michael in jail, or Angela and Summer being in situations they needed to get out of. David's constant patience and understanding gave his kids a better appreciation for everything he had done for them and they later joined him in working and planning all the celebrity events he was putting together, and did it with great pleasure.

Chapter 6:

Meeting the Master

CREATING A BOOK with someone is always an incredibly bonding experience. It was with Doris Day and our Doris Day companion and co-author, Gary McGee, and it certainly was an incredible experience with Mirisch.

Meeting David was a celebrity journey that started with Milt Suchin. At the beginning of the century I was assigned by Tony-nominated producer Jerry Goehring to create an American legend series for Connecticut through Sacred Heart University. I met Milt through this process.

We brought in stars like Shirley Jones, Mickey Rooney, and Debbie Reynolds. After finishing the series, I was brought back to Los Angeles and became executive director of the Jerry Pace Agency.

Milt Suchin introduced me to David Mirisch, who was producing several celebrity events and was possibly including some of our agency actors. We brought in Mikel Steven and Jenna McCombie, who would eventually become male and female celebrity bowling champions.

While working this event with David every year, I quickly discovered an appreciation for this great man who handled every event with calm, serenity, and great organizational skills. Stars loved him just as much as he loved them.

Together, we went from bowling tournaments to Pat Boone's golf tournaments to several other events, including with stars of major television series from *Criminal Minds* to *NCIS*.

David and I became good friends, as well his wife Sandy. As I got to know Sandy more and more I quickly realized she was his true champion. With her immense casting background and with David's promotional skill, they were a marriage made in heaven.

David Mirisch is one of those Hollywood veterans that rarely exist these days. David has a huge amount of respect from the Hollywood community and always remained scandal free.

David always gets things done and faces every obstacle in a very harmonious way and with a constant smile on his face.

Doing this book for me was a great discovery into a man that worked decade after decade with some of the biggest stars in Hollywood, but was never jaded by any of it. Doing every event with the biggest stars or the newest, treating all of them with equal importance; basically, making everyone feel so good and glad to be a part of anything he was doing.

David Mirisch Discovery - Snowboard Champ Hunter Wilson and LA Rams Cheerleader Michelle Turner Wilson with Agent Pierre Patrick at the Jerry Pace Agency

David Mirisch and Pierre Patrick

Celebrity Bowling Champions Mikel Steven and Jenna McCombie from *Hidden Valley: The Awakening* film with agent Pierre Patrick

Angela Mirisch

Michael Mirisch

Summer Mirisch

David and Sandy

Pierre Patrick is a writer, producer, and talent agency executive director of the Jerry Pace Agency in Beverly Hills. Born in Canada, and a long time member of the Recording and Television Academy (Grammys and Emmys), he produced the Grammy nominated album "The Christmas That Almost Wasn't" starring John Lithgow. Pierre has also written books for BearManor Media such as "Que Sera, Sera: The Magic of Doris Day" and "The Doris Day Companion: A Beautiful Day" with Garry McGee, and "Doris Day Paper Dolls Featuring 24 Fashions from Her Films" with David Wolfe. Pierre Patrick has had a long career working with celebrities ranging from Debbie Reynolds, Shirley Jones, Ben Vereen, Mickey Rooney, Ernest Borgnine and many others. In 2017, Pierre produced Jennifer Day's first album for Thump/Universal "Sweet Day Dreams". He is currently working on Hidden Valley: The Awakening, a feature film and series from the popular books written by Jon Morgan Woodward.

www.ingramcontent.com/pod-product-compliance
Lightning Source LLC
Chambersburg PA
CBHW070836100426

42813CB00003B/640